LENNON REMEMBERS

LENNON REMEMBERS

NEW EDITION

◆

JANN S. WENNER

VERSO

London • New York

A Rolling Stone Press Book
Editor: Holly George-Warren
Associate Editor: Kathy Huck
Assistant Editor: Wendy Mitchell
Editorial Assistant: Andrew Simon

This new edition first published by Verso 2000
© Rolling Stone Press 2000
Original edition first published in *Rolling Stone* 1971,
and in book form by Straight Arrow Books 1971
© Jann S. Wenner 1971
Verso
UK: 6 Meard Street, London W1V 3HR
USA: 180 Varick Street, New York NY 10014–4606

Verso is the imprint of New Left Books

ISBN 1–85984–600–9

British Library Cataloguing in Publication Data
A catalogue record for this book is
available from the British Library

Library of Congress Cataloging-in-Publication Data
A catalog record for this book is
available from the Library of Congress

Typeset by M Rules

Printed by R.R.Donnelley

John Lennon's handwritten lyrics—"God" © 1971 Lennon Music
and "Working Class Hero" © 1970 Lennon Music—are
reproduced courtesy of the Lennon Photo Archive

CONTENTS

"Forward" by Yoko Ono   vii

Introduction to the New Edition   ix

Introduction   xiii

Lennon Remembers   1

"FORWARD"

I'm often asked, "If John were here today, what do you think he would be doing?" I usually say something like, "Well, he was an Artist, and he had always been innovative. He liked to experiment with new media. So probably he would have loved the Internet. He always spoke of the coming of the Global Village. He would have been thrilled that now we really have it."

Reading this "revised" *Lennon Remembers* woke me up, though. ("Revised" somehow suggests it's a tamer version! *Hell!*) Now, I remember that John was a guy who was punk before Sid Vicious. A rapper before rap. What would John Lennon be doing now? Most likely, he would have joined the rappers, while plunging into the Internet at the same time. *Lennon Remembers* is classic Lennon. It's not a sit-back-and-put-your-feet-up read. You will probably feel like getting up and walking around the room after every paragraph. I did. It's a jolt on your nerves like bad, bad espresso. People with weak stomachs should close the window before reading. You might just feel like jumping out.

Politically incorrect? You need to experience John's words in the context of the times. In 1970, the whole world was against John, starting with his mates. Although we had been married for over a year, the media was still going crazy over it. He married a woman "eight years older" was the official running joke. "Dragon Lady" was the other. The *unofficial* one went from Jap to Chink to Bitch. Here's one example of the press "having fun" with us: A major magazine had a big article with a full-page ugly drawing of me, with John as a tiny beetle on a leash. "Rennon and his Excrusive Gloupie" was the title. John felt his wife had been slighted, to say the least. Generally, the world believed that John had gone insane. He felt choked. He kept trying to ignore the attacks and send good vibes to the world. The next year he would sing, "Imagine all the people living life in peace."

But in this 1970 interview, John is hitting back and doing a bad job of it. Not tactful, not calculated and, for once, not even particularly clever. Surprisingly, he is still sweet and funny throughout without trying. That was John. Get a whiff of his energy!

Reading this, I found myself skipping Jann's questions and my annoying little remarks. (Why did *we* have to say anything?!) Jann, the twenty-four-year-old genius, played the straight man for a change. I was the sidekick, laughing at the right *and* the wrong times. That was all we could do in the face of John's oratory, which went on without periods! There was no one like him and there never will be. And I miss him.

I hear John saying, "Okay, guys, shove this up your pretty whatever. You're all getting too comfortable."

Yoko Ono
July 2000

INTRODUCTION TO THE
NEW EDITION

Not having read *Lennon Remembers* since it was originally published in
ROLLING STONE in 1971, I was at first curious and enchanted upon
revisiting the interview, and then suddenly whipsawed back to a time
and place that I thought no longer existed. In retrospect, the interview
suffers from the still-developing skills of the interviewer—lack of both
methodology and a methodical approach—but perhaps that is one of
the very reasons the conversation with John Lennon, as well as the
extent of the encounter, was so passionate, unnerving and honest.
(I was twenty-four and John was thirty.) Rather than an in-depth discussion of old songs and times, what we have here is a candid, often
painful, running commentary on fresh and urgent matters, and a self-
portrait of the artist, the like of which I have not seen since.

I was very lucky in the early years of ROLLING STONE to be the ben-
eficiary of a friendship with John and Yoko. It began with ROLLING
STONE's publication of the naked *Two Virgins* pictures. We supported

them in their peace crusades and their solo records. In the process, we became one of their primary public outlets—all of which nourished and brought legitimacy and notice to the then-emerging ROLLING STONE. Through the course of this came the relationship that led to *Lennon Remembers*.

It's important to remember in reading this book that in 1970 the Beatles were the biggest phenomenon on earth—no kidding—"more popular than Jesus," in John's words. And there's been nothing like it since. The publication of these interviews was the first time that any of the Beatles, let alone the man who had founded the group and was their leader, finally stepped outside of that protected, beloved fairy tale and told the truth.

Primarily because of this need of John's to "gimme some truth," because he had just finished "primal" therapy, because he was bursting and bitter about the sugar-coated mythology of the Beatles and Paul McCartney's characterization of the breakup—and because he had a willing and sympathetic vehicle in me and ROLLING STONE—John poured forth here with all the spontaneity and urgency, and lack of caution, of doing it for the first time. *Lennon Remembers* overwhelms you with a real sense of the man, who he was and what he felt like, and the passion and the wit that he brought to nearly everything he did. Other than in some of his records, this interview is the only place I've had such a sense of John Lennon.

A great deal of the interview is so riveting ("The Beatles tours were like Fellini's *Satyricon*."), so direct ("Either I'm a genius or I'm mad, which is it?"), so colorful ("Paul said, 'Come and see the show.' I said, 'I read the news today, oh boy.'"), so intense and angry ("One has to completely humiliate oneself to be what the Beatles were."), that, at the risk of giving away what follows, I would like to suggest as a perspective the concluding questions and answers:

I have no more to ask.

Well, fancy that.

Do you have anything to add?

No, I can't think of anything positive and heartwarming to win your readers over.

Do you have a picture of "When I'm 64"?

No, no. I hope we're a nice old couple living off the coast of Ireland or something like that, looking at our scrapbook of madness.

For this new edition, the original tapes were re-transcribed with various bits and pieces added that had been deleted in the original publication for reasons of discretion (though that seems hard to believe), or errors in transcription due to the rushed circumstances at the time, as well as restoring Yoko's many comments and the as-taped order of the questions and answers. I am very grateful to Holly George-Warren, the conscientious editor and guardian of Rolling Stone Press, for supervising this project and doing the new edit herself.

All profits from this edition and all proceeds retroactively from past editions—and then some—have been given to gun control projects. I am grateful, of course, to Yoko Ono not only for arranging this interview in the first place but also for her consent to having it republished these many years later.

Jann S. Wenner
New York City
July 2000

INTRODUCTION

I did this interview with John Lennon in early December 1970, at the offices of his business manager, removed by high stories from the daytime traffic in the middle of the music business on Broadway in New York City. We were with Yoko, more or less isolated, in the massive walnut-paneled conference room.

Yoko was extremely helpful, adding a word here and there, providing a focus when uncertainties would develop. Because Yoko is a Beatle/John Lennon fan much like the rest of us, she was also unable to resist the laughter that arises from John's compulsive humor, and the awe at some of his statements and ideas; she shares and understands that good old Beatlemania.

Like all events and statements of a particular time, much of this interview has the intuitions and fads of the moment—Dr. Arthur Janov being an obvious example of one of those fads that has subsequently been bitterly denounced.

And I suspect John feels somewhat the same about this interview. Somewhere in here he passes on the warning that he's also just a cat who talks a lot and goes through many changes, leaving much of his prior statements behind him, theories that he's since discarded. Such is the nature of the maturing artist, constantly looking for new avenues and ideas.

The interview was the first time that voluble John poured it all out, or at least the major part of it, after the Beatles broke up. Regardless of his subsequent changes in specific ideas and views, it still holds as *the* statement about the end of the Beatles (because John was the leader of the group) and about John as an artist. It should be approached as history as well as revelation. A few parts, mainly factual material, were added by cassette tape on the phone at Christmastime.

I had wanted to add more to the interview, further discussions that would make the reminiscence complete and definitive, but along the way John lost interest. So what we present here is the event as it happened, slightly altered in retrospect and editing.

The interview was given mainly as a personal obligation (and partially as publicity for his about-to-be released solo album *John Lennon/Plastic Ono Band*), after about two or three years of dealings between myself and John, beginning with printing the *Two Virgins* picture in ROLLING STONE [November 23, 1968], then John's article on the Toronto Peace festival [April 16, 1970], and a two-hour meeting with Yoko at their house in Ascot when John refused to come downstairs to meet with me because, in Yoko's words, he was "too paranoid."

After many phone calls we finally met in June 1970 when he and Yoko came up to San Francisco for a visit during the time they were seeing Janov in Los Angeles. My wife, Jane, and I spent a weekend with them, showing them a little of San Francisco. The four of us went to see an empty afternoon theater showing of *Let It Be*, the filmic record of the final disinterest/dissolution of the Beatles. After the show—moved at whatever levels, either as participants or deep fans—we somehow cried.

About five months later, John and Yoko and I met up in New York to finally record his memories of the Beatles years.

John Lennon is one of the great artists of modern times. There are flaws in the interview, but here you have it: a remembrance of one of the most popular entertainers in history.

Jann S. Wenner
San Francisco
1971

GOD.

God is a concept by which we measure our pain
i'll say it again
God is a concept by which we measure our pain

i don't believe in magic
" "   " " iching
bible
tarot
hitler
jesus
kennedy
budda
mantra
gita
yoga
kings
Elvis
Dylan
Beatles

i just believe in me
and thats reality.
(Yoko and me).

art is fart

Peterowenunfairybo:

Peter Owen Unfairy to Yoko Ono.

i lost my art
at artschool

GROWING PAINS
for Yoko - who made it clear...

DEAD or ALIVE.
Before and after

Joan
of ARC.

voice bag.

would have thought
it would came to this.

Coloured TV. names of colenet)

water wiggle and slide. Julian
wham - 8.   & Kyoko

magic

I don't believe in i ching
tarot
bible

I just believe in me
and that's reality.

everywhere is somewhere
everyone is someone.

Rank & File
SKY WARN

mother card

i mother i

WORKING CLASS HERO

1) As soon as your born they make you feel small
by giving you no time instead of it all
till the pain so big you feel nothing at all
— working class etc =

2) they hurt you at home and they hit you at school
they hate you if your clever and they despise a fool
til your so fuckin cregy you can't falow their rules.
— working class etc. —

3) Keep you doped with religion and sex and t.v.
and you think your all clever and classless and free
but your still fucking peasants as far as I can see.
working class etc

4) When they've tortured and scared you for 20 odd years
then they expect you to pick a career
when you can't really function your so full of fear

5) there's room at the top they are telling you still
but first you must learn how to smile as you kill
if you want to be like the folks on the hill
a working class hero is something to be
" " " " " " " " "
if you want to be a hero well just follow me
" " " " " " " " " " "

as soon as your born they make you feel small
by giving you no time, instead of it all
till the pain so big you feel nothing at all
- a working class hero is something to be.

they ~~hurt~~ you at home and they hit you at school
they hate you if your clever and they despise a fool
till your so fuckin crazy you can't follow thirrules.
- a working class hero is something to be.

toffee nosed bourgoisee giving you loades
rubbing your face in their exercise books
being taught how to live by the biggest crooks.

keep you doped with religion and sex and T.V.
so you think your all clever and classless and free
but your still fucking peasant as far as I can see
oh oh oh oh oh
when they've tortured and scared you for 20 odd years
then they expect you to pick a career
when you can't really function your so full of fear
~~thworking class hero is something to do.~~
yes a working class hero is something to do.
if you want to be a hero well just follow me.

LENNON REMEMBERS

JOHN LENNON: Oh, you got notes and all that.

JANN WENNER: *Yeah.*

Well, we have to get it right, don't we? Gives me the paper to doodle on. When you get through the first one, I'll have it. Where to start? Don't be shy.

No, I'm not shy. Are you pleased with your new album?[1]

Yes. I'm very pleased. There's lots of things I would have liked to improve.

Like what?

I learned a lot on this album, technically, that I didn't have to learn so much before [because] there'd be George, Paul and I all listening to it and I wouldn't have to think so much about each individual sound.

---

[1] *John Lennon/Plastic Ono Band*, released by Apple/Capitol in 1970, was Lennon's first album after the Beatles' official break-up.

So there's a few things I learned about bass on one track or the other. Some technical things irritated me, but as a concept and as a whole thing, I'm pleased. If I get down to the nitty gritty, it'd drive me mad. But I like it. Otherwise I wouldn't have put it out.

When you record, do you go for feeling or for perfection of the sound?

Well, I like both. I go for feeling. Most takes are right off and most times I sang it and played it at the same time. I can't stand—

Overdubbing?

Putting the backing [first], which is what we used to do a lot in the old days. But [those tracks are] always dead. They'd gotten to that sort of dead Beatles sound or dead recording sound. Some of them are the second take or something, right off.

It starts out with bells. Why?

Well, I was watching TV *as usual* in California, and there was this old horror movie on. I just heard the bells, which sounded like that to me. But they were probably different cause those that I used on the album were actually other bells slowed down. I just thought, "That's how to start 'Mother.'" I knew "Mother" was going to be the first track.

You said you wrote most of the album in California?

Well, a lot of it. Actually I wrote "Mother" and "Isolation" in England. I finished them off in California. You have to push me if you want more detail—cause otherwise I'll just forget. "Look at Me" was written around the Beatles' double album time, but I just never got it done. There are a few like that lying round.

You said that this would be the first primal album.[2]

---

[2]   John and Yoko Ono began primal scream therapy with its originator Dr. Arthur Janov in April 1970.

When did I say that?

In California. Have you gone off that?

No, no, I haven't gone off it, it's just like primal is like another mirror, you know, and I just . . .

YOKO ONO: Because he, like any artist, really wants to be honest with himself and the albums. What he does is— instead of just patching up something that's *sort* of interesting—he really puts himself in it, his life in it. Like when he went to India and he was influenced by Maharishi and so forth.[3]

JOHN: It's like [how] writers take themselves to Singapore to get the atmosphere. So wherever I am . . . in that way it's a primal album, but is George's [*All Things Must Pass*] the first Gita album?[4] So it's that relevant.

YOKO: The primal scream is like a mirror, and he was looking at the mirror.

Let's talk about Arthur Janov for a second.[5] When you came out to San Francisco you wanted to do that advertisement [promoting primal scream therapy]. You wanted to say, "This is it."

Well, I think that's something people go through at the beginning of *that* therapy, cause you're so astounded at what you find out about yourself, you think, surely this is *something*. Because it happens to you,

---

3   Lennon and the other Beatles were adherents of the Maharishi Mahesh Yogi guru from 1967 to 1968, and spent time on Maharishi's ashram in India in 1968, studying transcendental meditation.

4   George Harrison continued to study Indian spirituality, including the *Bhagavad-Gita*.

5   The psychologist who created primal scream therapy, which helped patients overcome problems by reliving childhood pain, then releasing pain with crying and screaming.

you think, well this must be the first time it's happened. So I was just full of it, like that. Also, I need to have a reason for going somewhere, otherwise I'm too nervous. So I conned meself, and that was a good way of coming to San Francisco [*laugh*] to see you. Then I have an objective: I'm going to do an advert . . . Then we settle down, we just talk. So it's really like that. But I still think the therapy's great, but I just don't want to make it into a big Maharishi thing. You were right to tell me, "Forget the advert." And that's why I don't even want to talk too much about it. If people know what I've been through there, and if they want to find out, they can find out. Otherwise it turns into *that* again.

Yeah. So you no longer feel that this is the single thing to do, but just one of a number of therapies—

I don't know, because I've no idea about any other therapy. I don't think anything else would work on me so well. But then of course I'm not through with it. It's a process that's going on—we primal almost daily. And the only difference—I don't really want to get this big primal thing going because it gets so *embarrassing*. And in a nutshell, primal therapy allowed us to feel feelings continually, and those feelings usually make you cry. That's all. Before I wasn't feeling things—I was having blocks to the feelings, and the feelings come through, you cry. It's as simple as that really.

Do you think the experience of therapy helped you become a better singer?

Oh no.

Do you think your singing is better on this album?

Well, it's probably better because I've got the whole time to meself. I'm pretty good at home with me tapes [*laugh*]. But this time it was *my* album. It used to get a bit embarrassing in front of George and Paul cause we know each other so well: "Oh, he's trying to be Elvis, oh he's doing this now," you know. We're a bit supercritical of each other. So we inhibited each other a lot. And now I had Yoko there and Phil [Spector][6] there, alternatively and together, who sort of love me, okay, so I can perform better. And I relaxed. I've got a studio at home now and I think it'll be better next time cause that's even less inhibiting than going to EMI [Studios]. It's like that. The looseness of the singing was developing on "Cold Turkey" from the experience of Yoko's singing—she does not inhibit her throat.[7]

It says on the album that Yoko does "wind."

Yeah. Well, she plays wind. She played the atmosphere.

YOKO: I was around.

JOHN: No, she wasn't *around*, she has a musical ear and she can produce rock & roll. She can produce me, which she did for some of the tracks when Phil couldn't come at first. I'm not going to start saying that she did this and he did that. You don't have to have been born and bred in rock. She knows when a bass sound's right and when the guy's playing out of rhythm and when the engineer . . . She has a bit of trouble, the engineer thinks, "Well, who the hell's this—what does *she* know about it?"

"Working Class Hero" sounds like an early Dylan song.

Well, anybody that sings with a guitar and just sings about something heavy will tend to sound like Dylan. I'm bound to be influenced

---

[6]   The legendary producer responsible for the "Wall of Sound" style of production that he pioneered with girl groups beginning in 1961. Spector co-produced *Plastic Ono Band* with John and Yoko.

[7]   "Cold Turkey" was a single that Plastic Ono Band released in October 1969.

by [those] because that's the only kind of really folk music I ever listened to. I never liked the fruity Judy Collins and [Joan] Baez and all that stuff. So the only folk music I know is those [*sings*] about miners up in Newcastle. Or Dylan. So in that way I've been influenced, but it doesn't sound like Dylan to me. Does it sound like Dylan to you?

Only in the instrumentation . . . the acoustic guitar strumming.

But that's the only way to play, you know, you go *jing-jing-a-jing-a-jing-jing-a*—I never listened that hard to him, you know?

What's November 5th?[8]

In England it's the day they blew up the Houses of Parliament. We celebrate it by having bonfires every November the 5th. It was just an ad lib. It was about the third take, and it begins to sound like Frankie Laine—when you're singing [*sings*] "remember, remember, the 5th of November." And I just broke and it went on for about another seven or eight minutes. I was just ad libbing and goofing about. But then I cut it there and it just exploded cause it was a good joke. Haven't you ever heard of Guy Fawkes?

Guy Fawkes, that's Guy Fawkes Day?

That's Guy Fawkes Day, yeah. And I thought it was just poignant that we should blow up the Houses of Parliament [*laugh*].

Do you get embarrassed sometimes when you hear the album, when you think about how personal it is?

No—sometimes I can hear it and be embarrassed, just by the performance or by the music or by the statements. And sometimes I *don't*.

---

[8] A reference in "Working Class Hero" to the date in 1605 when conspirators plotted to blow up England's Houses of Parliament.

I change daily. Just before it's coming out, I can't bear to hear it in the house, or play it anywhere. But a few months before that I can play it to everyone. It just changes all the time. Sometimes I used to listen to something, I don't know, Buddy Holly or anything, one day the record would sound twice as fast as the next day. Did you ever experience that on a single? I used to have that, like "Hound Dog" or something, one day it'd sound very slow and one day it would sound very fast. And it was just the mood, just my feeling towards it. The way I heard it. So it can do that. But that's where you've got to make your artistic judgment to say, "Well this is the take and this isn't." That's where you have to make the decision when it sounds reasonable.

What is your concept of pain?

I don't know what you mean really.

The song "God" starts out by saying "God is a concept by which we measure our pain."

Our pain is the pain we go through all the time. You're born in pain, and pain is what we're in most of the time. And I think that the bigger the pain, the more gods we need.

There's a tremendous body of philosophic literature about God as a measurement of pain.

Oh, I never heard about it. See, it was my own revelation. I don't know who wrote about it or what anybody else said. I just know that's what *I* know. Amazing.

YOKO: You just felt it.

JOHN: Yeah, I felt it, you see. So when I felt it, it's like I *was* crucified. So I know what they're talking about now.

What's the difference between the producing styles of George Martin and Phil Spector?[9]

Well, George Martin—I don't know. You see, for quite a few of our albums, like the Beatles' double album, George Martin didn't really produce it. I don't know whether this is standard but he didn't, I can't remember. In the early days I can remember what George Martin did.

What did he do?

He would translate. If Paul wanted to use violins and that, he would translate it for him. Like in "In My Life," there's an Elizabethan piano solo in it. So he would do things like that. I would say, "Play it like Bach or something, could you put twelve bars in there?" And he helped us develop a language a little, to talk to musicians. Because I'm very shy and [for] many, many reasons, I didn't very much go for musicians. I didn't like to have to go and see twenty guys sitting there and try to tell them what to do. Because they were always so lousy anyway. So apart from the early days, I didn't have much to do with it. I did it meself.

Why do you use Phil now instead of George?

Well, it's not *instead* of George Martin. I would not *use* anybody. That's nothing personal against George Martin, he just doesn't—he's more Paul's style of music than mine.

Did Phil make any special contributions?

Phil—yes, yes. You can hear Spector here and there. There's no specifics, you can just hear him. Because Phil is, I believe, a great artist. But like all great artists, he's very neurotic. But we've done quite a few tracks together, Yoko and I, and she'd be encouraging me in the other

[9]   George Martin signed the Beatles to Parlophone/EMI in 1962 and became their longtime producer.

room and all that. And we were just lagging, and Phil moved in and brought in a new life to it because we were getting heavy. We'd done a few things, and the thrill of recording had worn off a little.

What do you think of the album overall?

I think it's the best thing I've ever done. I think it's realistic and it's true to the *me* that has been developing over the years from "In My Life," "I'm a Loser," "Help!," "Strawberry Fields." They were all personal records. I always wrote about me and didn't really enjoy writing third-person songs about people who lived in concrete flats and things. I like first-person music. But because of hangups and many other things, I would only now and then specifically write about me. And now I wrote *all* about me, and that's why I like it. It's *me*, and nobody else. So I like it.

There's an honesty to it . . .

It's real, you know. It's about me, and I don't know about anything else really. The only true songs I ever wrote were "Help!" and "Strawberry Fields." And I can name a few, I can't think of them offhand, that I always considered my best songs. They were the ones that I really wrote from experience and not projecting myself into a situation and writing a nice story about it, which I always found phony. But I'd find occasion to do it because I've had to produce so much work or because I'd be so hung up I couldn't even think about myself.

On this album there's practically no imagery at all . . .

No. Because there was none in my head. There were no hallucinations.

There's no "newspaper taxi" . . .

No, I was consciously writing poetry then, and that's self-conscious poetry. But the poetry on this album is superior to anything I've done because it's not self-conscious in that way. I had *least* trouble writing the songs of all time.

YOKO: There's no bullshit.

JOHN: Yeah, no bullshit.

The music is very simple and very sparse . . .

Well, I always liked simple rock. There's a great one in England now, "I Hear You Knocking."[10] And I liked "Spirit in the Sky" a few months back.[11] I always liked simple rock and nothing else. I was influenced by acid and got psychedelic, like the whole generation, but really, I like rock & roll. I express myself best in rock, and I had a few ideas to do *this* with "Mother" and *that* with "Mother," but the piano does it all for you. Your mind can do the rest of it. I think the backings on [my record] are as complicated as the backings on any record you've ever heard. If you've got an ear, you can hear. *Any* musician will tell you, just play a note on a piano, it's got a lot of harmonics in it. So it got to that. What the hell, it didn't need anything else.

How did you put together that litany in "God"?

What's litany?

The "I don't believe in magic," how the song starts off.

Well, like a lot of the words, they just came out of me mouth. It started off like that. "God" was stuck together from three songs almost. I had the idea, "God is the concept by which we measure our pain." So when you have a [phrase] like that, you just sit down and sing the first tune that comes into your head. And the tune is the simple [*sings*]

---

[10]   Dave Edmunds' 1970 hit remake of Smiley Lewis' 1955 song.

[11]   Norman Greenbaum's one and only hit, which rose to Number Three on the U.S. charts in 1969.

"God is the concept—*bomp-bomp-bomp-bomp*" cause I like that kind of music. And then I just rolled into it. [*Sings*] "I don't believe in magic"— and it was just going on in me head. And "I Ching" and "the Bible," the first three or four just came out, whatever came out.

When did you know that you were going to be working toward the line "I don't believe in Beatles"?

I don't know when I realized I was putting down all these things I didn't believe in. I could have gone on, it was like a Christmas card list—where do I end? Churchill, and who have I missed out? It got like that and I thought I had to stop. . . . I was going to leave a gap and say, just fill in your own, for whoever you don't believe in. It just got out of hand. But Beatles was the final thing because it's like I no longer believe in myth, and Beatles is another myth. I don't believe in it. The dream's over. I'm not just talking about the Beatles is over, I'm talking about the generation thing. The dream's over, and I have personally got to get down to so-called reality.

When did you become aware that "God" would be the song played the most on the radio?

Well, I didn't know that. They started off playing "Look at Me" because it was easy and they probably thought it was the Beatles or something. So I don't know, if that is the one, well that's the one. "God" and "Working Class Hero" probably are the best sort of ideas or feelings on the record.

In "God," why did you choose to refer to Dylan as Zimmerman rather than Dylan?

Because *Dylan* is bullshit. Zimmerman is his name. I don't believe in Dylan—I don't believe in Tom Jones, either, in that way. Zimmerman is his name. My name isn't John Beatle, it's John Lennon. Just like that.

Why did you tag "My Mummy's Dead" at the end?

Because that's what's happened. All these songs just came out of me. I didn't sit down to think, "I'm going to write about my mother" or I didn't sit down to think, "I'm going to write about this, that or the other." They all came out, like all the best work of anybody's ever does. All these came out because I had the time. If you're on holiday or in therapy and you spend the time—like in India, where I could write a lot, I wrote the last batch of my best songs. "I'm So Tired" and "Yer Blues" were pretty sort of realistic.[12] They were about me, and they always struck me as—not, what's the word? Funny . . . ironic?—that I was writing supposedly in the presence of [a] guru and meditating so many hours a day, writing, "I'm So Tired" . . .

Songs of pain.

Songs of such pain as "Yer Blues," which I meant. I was trying to express it in blues idiom cause . . .

YOKO: "Cold Turkey" too.

JOHN: "Cold Turkey." I was in Maharishi's camp writing "I want to die . . ."

Was "Yer Blues" also deliberately meant to be a parody of the English blues thing?

No—well a bit, because I'm a bit—we all are self-conscious. And the Beatles are super self-conscious people about parodying Americans, which we do and have done. I know we developed our own style, but we still in a way parody American music. This is interesting because in the early days in England all the groups were like Elvis and a backing group.

---

[12] Both songs are on the Beatles' 1968 self-titled double album, known as the "White Album."

And the Beatles deliberately didn't move like Elvis. That was our policy because we found it stupid and bullshit. And then Mick Jagger came out and resurrected bullshit movement, wiggling your ass and that. So then people began to say, "The Beatles are passé because they don't move." But we did it as an intellectual—when we were younger, we used to move, we used to jump around, do all the things they're doing now, like going onstage with toilet seats and shitting and pissing, that's what we were doing in Hamburg. And smashing things up. It wasn't a thing that Pete Townshend sort of worked out, it's something that you do when you play six or seven hours. There's nothing else to do, you smash the place up, you insult everybody. But we were groomed, and we dropped all that, and whatever it was we started off talking about—which was what? About singing—what was it? What was the beginning of that?

That "Yer Blues" was deliberately parodying . . .

Yeah, yeah, so there's a self-consciousness about suddenly singing blues. We were all listening to Sleepy John Estes and all that in art school, like everybody else. But to sing it was something else. And so I was self-conscious about doing it. I think Dylan does it a lot. In case he's not sure of himself, he makes it a double entendre, so therefore you're secure in your hipness. But Paul was saying, "Don't call it 'Yer Blues,' just say it straight." But I was self-conscious and I went for "Yer Blues." But I think all that is past now, because we've all got over it, *that* self-consciousness.

YOKO: I think John being John is a bit unfair to his music in a way. I'd like to just add a few things. He can go on for an hour or something, but I mean one thing is, like about Arthur Janov. Say if John fell in love, you know, he's always falling in love with all sorts of things— Maharishi, whatnot . . . I just think that he just goes on falling in love with all sorts of things. But, say, he fell in love with some girl or something and he wrote a song; who he fell in love with is not very important, it's the outcome of it, the song itself is important.

You would have to say that a song like "Well, Well, Well" is connected with primal therapy.

JOHN: Why?

YOKO: Why?

The screams.

JOHN: No, no, but listen to "Cold Turkey."

YOKO: Well, he's screaming already there.

JOHN: Listen to "Twist and Shout." I couldn't sing the damn thing, I was just screaming. Listen to "A-wop-bop-a-loo-wop-a-wop-bam-boom."[13] Don't get the therapy confused with the music.

YOKO: *I* was screaming.

JOHN: And Yoko's whole thing was that scream. Listen to "Don't Worry Kyoko." It's one of the fuckin' best rock & roll records ever made. Listen to it and play "Tutti Frutti." Listen to "Don't Worry Kyoko," the other side of "Cold Turkey." I'm digressing for a moment, but if somebody with a rock-oriented mind can possibly listen to her stuff, you'll see what she's doing. It's fantastic. It's as important as anything we ever did and as important as anything the Stones or Townshend ever did. Listen to it, and you'll hear what she's puttin' down. And on "Cold Turkey," I'm getting towards it. I'm influenced by her music one thousand percent more than I ever was by Dylan. She makes music like you've never heard on earth. And when the musicians play with it, they're inspired out of their

---

[13] A line from Little Richard's first hit, "Tutti Frutti," which was released in late 1955.

skulls. I don't know how much they play it later . . . We've got a cut of her from the Lyceum in London with thirty—fifteen or twenty musicians playing with her, from Bonnie and Delaney and the fuckin' lot. We played the tracks the other night, and it's the most fantastic music I've ever heard. They've probably gone away and forgotten all about it. We're gonna put it out. It's *fantastic*! It's twenty years ahead of its time. There's a track with Ornette Coleman from the past that we put on [the record] to show people that Yoko wasn't discovered by the Beatles, that she's been around a few years. We've got stuff of her with [John] Cage, Ornette Coleman that we're putting out. We're going to put *Oldies but Goldies* out next for Yoko. Anyway, back to mine.

When you talked about "Cold Turkey," you said, "That's not a song, that's a diary."

JOHN: Yeah, well so is this.

YOKO: Everything.

JOHN: So is this. And I announced "Cold Turkey" at the Lyceum, saying, "I'm gonna sing a song about pain." So pain and screaming was before Janov. I went through therapy, like I told you, with him. And I'm probably looser all over.

Are you less paranoid now?

No, but I can feel my own fear, I can feel my own pain. Therefore, I can handle it better than I could before. That's all. I'm the same. Only there's a channel. It doesn't just remain in me. It goes round, and I can move a little easier.

What was your experience with heroin?

Heroin. It just was not too much fun. I never injected it. We sniffed a little when we were in real pain. I mean we just couldn't—people were giving us such a hard time—

YOKO: We didn't get into it so much.

JOHN: No. But we got such a hard time from everyone. And I've had so much shit thrown at me and especially at Yoko. People like Peter Brown in our office, he comes down and shakes my hand and doesn't even say hello to her.[14] Now that's going on all the time. And we get in so much pain that we have to do something about it. And that's what happened to us. We took H because of what the Beatles and their pals were doing to us. And we got out of it. They didn't set down to do it, but things came out of that period. And I don't forget.

YOKO: Let's go back to what he was saying about Phil Spector. I mean John really produced his own stuff. Like Phil is, as you know, well known as a very skillful sort of technician in electronics and engineering and all that.

JOHN: But let's not take away from what he did do, which was bring a lot of energy and taught me a *lot*. And I would use him again.

YOKO: Yes, but he's so *definite* about things.

JOHN: I know what I want, you see. When I say to Phil, "I want this," he gets it for me like *that* [*snaps fingers*].

YOKO: There's a lot of Spector sound in it . . .

JOHN: You can hear Spector on the album.

You can hear the voices the way Spector . . .

JOHN: No, he—no, no, that was me. I did that before Phil came. I did quite—quite a lot of it before he came.

---

[14]   Peter Brown was the Beatles' manager Brian Epstein's assistant, who later served as Director of Apple Corps.

YOKO: And also that "Mother" bell, he was saying, "It's a church bell and it's connected with his childhood." He was always saying, "Sundays I heard church bells."

JOHN: Yeah, I read an article on some new Southern country singer who wrote something like "Sunday's a lonely day."[15] Okay.

On your past records, like "Sgt. Pepper's," it's "Come and see the show" and this record's so personal . . .

Paul said, "Come and see the show." I didn't. I said, "I read the news today, oh boy," that's what I said. I'm "Mr. Kite," mind you.

You're "Mr. Kite"?

No, no. I wrote that as a pure poetic job, to write a song sitting there. I had to write because it was time to write. And I had to write it quick because otherwise I wouldn't have been on the album [*laugh*]. So I had to knock off a few songs. I knocked off "A Day in the Life," or my section of it, and whatever we were talking about, "Mr. Kite," or something like that. I was very paranoid in those days, I could hardly move.

I read that little interview done at the time when you went to the Rock & Roll Revival in Toronto and you said you were throwing up before you went onstage . . .

Yeah, I was. We were full of junk too. I just threw up for hours till I went on. I nearly threw up in "Cold Turkey"—I had a review in ROLLING STONE about the film of it—which I haven't seen yet, and they're saying, "I was this and that." And I was throwing up nearly in the number, I could hardly sing any of them, I was full of shit.

Would you still be that nervous if you appeared in public?

---

[15] Lennon is possibly referring to Kris Kristofferson, who wrote "Sunday Morning Coming Down" in 1969.

Always that nervous, but with one thing and another [*laugh*], it just had to come out some way. I don't think I'll do much appearing. It's not worth the strain. I don't want to perform *too* much for people.

What do you think of George's album?

I don't know, I think it's *alright*. [pause] At home, I wouldn't play that kind of music, but I don't want to hurt George's feelings. I mean I don't know how to say about it. I think it's better than Paul's.

What do you think of Paul's?

I thought Paul's was rubbish. I think he'll make a better one when he's frightened into it. But I thought that first one was light and whatever. But when I listen to the radio and I hear George's stuff coming over, well then it's pretty goody-good. It's like that. But my personal tastes are very strange.

What do your personal tastes run to?

"Wop bop a loo bop." You know? I mean I like rock & roll, man, I— I don't like much else.

Why rock & roll?

That's the music that inspired me to play music. There's nothing conceptually better than rock & roll. No group, be it Beatles, Dylan or Stones, has ever improved on "Whole Lotta Shakin' [Goin' On]" for my money.[16] Maybe I'm like our parents, that's my period. I dig it and I'll never leave it.

What do you think of the rock & roll scene today?

I don't know what it is. You'd have to name it.

Do you get any pleasure out of the Top Ten? Do you listen to the Top Ten?

---

[16]   Jerry Lee Lewis' signature song from 1957.

No, I never listen, only when I'm recording or about to bring something out. And I'll listen, just before I record, to a few albums to see what people are doing, if they improved any or if anything has happened. And nothing's really happened. There's a lot of great guitarists and musicians around, but nothing's happening. I mean I don't like the Blood, Sweat and Tears shit—I think all that is bullshit. Rock & roll is doing like jazz, as far as I can see. And the bullshitters are going off into that excellentness, which I never believed in. I consider myself in the avant garde of rock & roll, because Yoko taught me a lot and I taught her a lot. And I think on her album, you can hear it. If I can get away from her album for a minute.

What did you think of Dylan's album?[17]

I thought it wasn't much, because I expect more. Maybe I expect too much from people, but I expect more. I haven't been a Dylan follower since he stopped rocking. I like "Rolling Stone" and the few things he did then. I like a few things he did in the early days, but the rest of it's just like McCartney or something. It's no different—it's a myth.

You don't think then that it's a legitimate "new morning"?

No, it's a lot of bullshit. It might be a new morning for him because he's stopped singing on the top of his—[*demonstrates*] high up there. And he's singing down there [*demonstrates*]. I mean it's alright, but it's nothing. It doesn't mean a fucking thing. I'd sooner have "I Hear You Knocking" by Dave Edmunds that's top [of the charts] in England now. [*Sings*] "You went away and left me a long time ago"—all that.

---

[17] *New Morning*, released in 1970.

It's strange that George comes out with this Hare Krishna Gita LP. And you come out with the opposite. How do you think George will react to that?

Well, I don't know. I can't imagine what George thinks. But I suppose he thinks I've lost the way, or something like that. But to me I'm home. I'll never change much from this.

Let's reapproach that. The Beatles were talked about as being four parts of the same person. What's happened to those four parts?

They remembered that they were four individuals. You see, we believed the Beatles myth, too. I don't know whether the others still believe it, but we were four guys that—I met Paul and said, "Do you want to join me band?" and then George joined and then Ringo joined. We were just a *band* who made it very, very big—that's all. Our best work was never recorded.

Why?

Because we were performers in spite of what Mick [Jagger] says about us, in Liverpool, Hamburg and around the dance halls. What we generated was fantastic when we played straight rock, and there was nobody to touch us in Britain. But as soon as we made it, the edges were knocked off. Brian Epstein put us in suits and all that, and we made it very, very big. We sold out. The music was dead before we even went on the theater tour of Britain. We were feeling shit already, because we had to reduce an hour or two hours' play—and which we were glad [to do] in one way—to twenty minutes, and go on and repeat the same twenty minutes every night. The Beatles' music died then, as musicians. That's why we never improved as musicians. We killed ourselves then to make it—and that was the end of it. George and I are more inclined to say that. We always missed the club dates cause that's when we were playing music. Then later on we became technically efficient recording artists, which was another thing. Because we were competent people, whatever media you put us in, we can produce something worthwhile.

How do you rate yourself as a guitarist? As a musician?

Well, it depends what kind of guitarist . . .

Rock & roll.

I'm okay. I'm not technically very good, but I can make it fucking howl and move. I was rhythm guitarist, and it's an important job. I can make a band drive.

How do you rate George?

He's pretty good. I prefer meself—I have to be honest. I'm really very embarrassed about my guitar playing in one way because it's very poor. I can never move. But I can make a guitar speak. I think there's a guy called Ritchie Valens—no, Richie Havens? Did he play very strange guitar? He's a black guy that was on at the Isle of Wight concert, sang "Strawberry Fields" or something.

Oh, Richie Havens.

Yeah, he plays like one chord all the time—pretty funky guitar. He doesn't seem to be able to play in the real sense. I'm like that. But Yoko's made me get cocky about me guitar cause she keeps saying— Okay, see, one part of me says, "Yes, of course I can play because I can make a rock move." But the other part of me says, "Well, I wish I could just do it like B.B. King." If you put me with B.B., I'll feel *silly*. But I'm an artist and if you give me a tuba, I'll bring you something out of it.

You said that you can make the guitar speak. In which songs do you feel you've done that?

"I Found Out," I think it's nice. It drives along. I don't know, ask Eric Clapton, he thinks I can play [*laugh*]. A lot of you people want the technical thing, then you think, oh, well that's like wanting technical films. Most critics of rock & roll and guitarists are in the stage of the Fifties where they wanted a technically perfect film finished for them and then they would feel happy. I'm a cinéma-vérité guitarist-musician. You have to break down your barriers to be able to hear what I'm playing. There's a nice little bit I played on *Abbey Road*. Paul gave us each a piece, a little break where Paul plays, George plays and I play. When you listen to it you know . . .

Which is that?

There's one bit, one of those where it stops, on "Carry That Weight," then suddenly it goes *boom-boom-boom* on the drums and we all take it in turns to play. I'm the third one on it. I have a definite style of playing, always had. But I was overshadowed. They call George the invisible singer, I'm the invisible guitarist.

You said you played the obbligato on "Get Back"?

I played the solo on that, yeah. When Paul was feeling kind, he'd give me a solo. Maybe if he was feeling guilty that he'd had most of the A sides or something, he'd give me a solo. And I played the solo on that. I think George produces some beautiful guitar playing, but I think he's too hung up to really let go. But so is Eric, really. Maybe he's changed. They're all so hung up. Well, we all are, that's the problem. But I really like B.B. King.

Do you like Ringo's record? His country one?

I think it's a good record. I wouldn't buy any of it. I think it's a good record and I was pleasantly surprised to hear "Beaucoups of Blues," that song. I felt good. I was glad and I didn't feel as embarrassed as I did about his first record. But it's hard for you to ask me—it's like asking me what do I think of . . . ask me about other people. Because it looks so awful when I say, "I don't like this and I don't like that." It's just that, I don't like many of the Beatles records either. My own taste is different from that which I've played sometimes, which is called "cop-out," to make money or whatever. Or because I didn't know any better.

I'd like to ask you more questions about Paul and go through that. We saw 'Let It Be' in San Francisco.[18] What were your feelings about that?

I felt sad. That film was set up by Paul, for Paul. That's one of the main reasons the Beatles ended, cause . . . I can't speak for George, but I pretty damn well know, we got fed up with being sidemen for Paul. After Brian died, that's what began to happen to us.[19] And the camera work was set up to show Paul and not to show anybody else. That's how I felt about it. And on top of that, the people that cut it, cut it as "Paul is God" and we're just lying around there. And that's what I felt. I knew there was some shots of Yoko and me that had been just chopped out of the film for no other reason than the people were oriented towards Engelbert Humperdinck. I felt sick.

How would you trace the breakup of the Beatles?

---

[18] *Let It Be* was a film documenting the Beatles' 1969 recording sessions and their final live performance.

[19] Brian Epstein died in August 1967 from an overdose of prescription medication.

After Brian died, we collapsed. Paul took over and supposedly led us, you know. But what is leading us when we went round in circles? We broke up then. That was the disintegration.

When did you first feel that the Beatles had broken up?

I don't remember. I was in my own pain. I wasn't noticing really. I just did it like a job. The Beatles broke up after Brian died. We made the double album, the set. It's like if you took each track off and put all mine and all George's. It's just like I told you many times, me and a backing group, Paul and a backing group. And I enjoyed it. But we broke up then.

Where were you when you heard Brian died?

We were in Wales with Maharishi. We'd just gone down after seeing his lecture the first night. And we went down to Wales and we heard it then. And then we went right off into the Maharishi thing.

Where were you?

A place called Bangor in Wales . . .

In a hotel?

No, we were just outside a lecture hall with Maharishi. It just sort of came over. Somebody came up to us—the press were there cause we'd gone down with this strange Indian. And they said, "Brian's dead." I was stunned. We all were. And the Maharishi—we went into him, "He's dead," and all that. And he was sort of saying, "Oh, forget it, be happy." Fucking *idiot*. Like parents: "Smile." That's what Maharishi said. So we did. And we went along with the Maharishi trip.

What was your feeling when Brian died? Do you remember?

The feeling that anybody has when somebody close to them dies. There's a sort of little hysterical sort of "hee-hee, I'm glad it's not me," or *something* in it, that funny feeling when somebody dies. I don't know whether you've had it. I've had *a lot* of people die on me. And the other feeling is, "What the fuck? What can I do?" I knew that we were in trouble then. I didn't really have any misconceptions about our ability to do anything other than play music. And I was scared. I thought, "We've fuckin' had it."

What were the events that immediately happened after Brian died?

Well, we went with Maharishi. I remember being in Wales and then I can't remember. I'll probably have to have a bloody [primal] session to remember it. I can't remember. It just all happened.

Then you went to India.

Yeah, I think so.

What about the funeral?

Oh, that was bullshit. I was offended enough that I've forgotten. Funerals are . . .

And how did Paul . . .

I don't know how the others took it. I can never tell how, it's no good asking me. It's like me asking how you took it—I don't know. I'm in my own head, I can't be in anybody else's. I don't know what George, Paul and Ringo think any more than I do about . . . I know them pretty well, but I don't know anybody *that* well. Yoko I know about the best. I don't know how they felt. I was in my own thing. We were all just like dazed.

So Brian died and then what happened is Paul started to take over?

I don't know how much of this I want to put out, I'll tell you. I think Paul had an impression—he has it now, like a parent, that we should be thankful for what he did, for keeping the Beatles going. But when you look upon it objectively, he kept it going for his *own* sake. Not for my sake did Paul struggle. But Paul made an attempt to carry on as if Brian hadn't died. By saying, "Now, now, boys, we're going to make a record." And being the kind of person I am, I thought, "Well, you know, we're going to make a record, alright." So I went along, we went and made a record. And I suppose we made *Pepper*, I'm not sure.

That was before.

That was before Brian. Oh, I see. Well, we made the double album then. But it was like that, you know. Was *Magical Mystery Tour* after Brian? Paul had a tendency to just come along and say, "Well, [I've] written ten songs, let's record now." And I said, "Give us a few days and I'll knock a few off." Or something like that. He came and showed me what his idea was for *Magical Mystery Tour* and this is how it went, it went round like this, the story and production, and he said, "Here's the segment, you write a little piece for that." And I thought, "Fuckin' hell, I've never made a film, what's he mean?" He said, "Write a script." So I ran off and wrote the dream sequence for the fat woman and all the things—the spaghetti and all that. So it was like that. George and I were sort of grumbling, "Fuckin' movie, well we better do it." A feeling that we owed the public to do these things. So we made it.

When did your songwriting partnership with Paul end?

That ended, I don't know, around 1962 or something. If you give me the albums, I can tell you exactly who wrote what, and which line. We sometimes wrote together and sometimes didn't. But all our best work—apart from the early days, like "I Want to Hold Your Hand," we wrote together, and things like that—we wrote apart always. Even "One After 909" on the whatsit LP, it's one I wrote when I was seventeen or eighteen in Liverpool separately from Paul. "The Sun Is Fading Away" and things like that Paul wrote. We always wrote separately. But we wrote together because we enjoyed it a lot sometimes and also because they'd say, "You're going to make an album." We'd get together and knock off a few songs. Just like a job.

Whose idea was it to go to India?

I don't know. Probably George's, I have no idea. We [John and Yoko] met around then. I was going to take [Yoko], but I lost me nerve because I was going to take me wife *and* Yoko and I didn't know how to work it [*laugh*]. So, I didn't do it. I didn't quite do it.

You wrote "Sexy Sadie" about the Maharishi.

That's about Maharishi, yeah. I copped out and wouldn't write "Maharishi, what have you done, you made a fool of everyone." [leaning into mike of tape recorder] But now it can be told, fab listeners.

When did you realize that he was making a fool of you?

I don't know, I just sort of saw.

While in India, or when you got back?

Yeah, there was a big hullabaloo about him trying to rape Mia Farrow or trying to get off with Mia Farrow and a few other women, things like that. And we went down to him and we'd stayed up all night discussing, was it true or not true. And when George started thinking it might be true, I thought, "Well it must be true, cause if George is doubting it, there must be something in it." So we went to see Maharishi, the whole gang of us the next day charged down to his hut, his very rich-looking bungalow in the mountains. And I was the spokesman—as usual, when the dirty work came, I actually had to be leader, whatever the scene was, when it came to the nitty gritty I had to do the speaking. And I said, "We're leaving."

"Why?" Hee-hee, all that shit. And I said, "Well if you're so cosmic, you'll know why." He was always intimating, and there were all his right hand men intimating that he did miracles. He said, "I don't know why, you must tell me." And I just kept saying "You know why"—and he gave me a look like, "I'll kill you, bastard." He gave me such a look, and I knew then when he looked at me, because I'd called his bluff. And I was a bit rough to him.

YOKO: You were expecting too much from him.

JOHN: I always do. I always expect too much. I'm always expecting my mother and don't get her, that's what it is. Or some parents. I know that much.

But when did you decide you had to come to New York and denounce the Maharishi?

Denounce him?

Well, you came to New York and had that press conference.

The Apple thing, that was to announce Apple.[20]

Right. But also at the same time—

I don't remember that. Well, what did I say? I don't know. We all say a lot of things that we don't know what we're talking about. I'm probably doing it now. I don't know what I said. See, everybody takes you up on the words you said the night before. I'm just a guy who people ask "what about" things. I blab off, and some of it makes sense, some of it's bullshit. And some of it's lies and some of it's God knows what I'm saying. I don't know what I said about Maharishi. All I know is what we said about Apple, which is worse.

Let's talk about Apple.

[20]   In 1967 the Beatles started their own company, Apple Corps, with five creative divisions, including the Apple record label. They publicly offered to assist aspiring artists, and according to Derek Taylor, the Beatles' publicist, "the promise was that all sincere supplicants would be given encouragement, succour, a contract and maybe an envelope full of money."

Alright.

How did that start?

Clive Epstein or some other such business freak came up to us and said, "You got to spend so much money or the tax'll take it.[21] We're thinking of opening a chain of retail clothes," or some barmy thing like that. And we were all muttering about, "Well, if we're going to have to open a shop, let's open something we're interested in." We went through all these different ideas about this, that and the other. Paul had a nice idea about opening up white houses where it would sell white china and things like that, everything white because you can never get anything white, which is pretty groovy. It didn't end up with that, it ended up with Apple, with all this junk and The Fool and all the stupid clothes and all that.[22]

When did you decide to close that down?

I don't know, I was controlling the scene at the time; I mean I was the one going in the office and shouting. Paul had done it for six months, I walked in and changed everything. But there were all the Peter Browns reporting behind me back to Paul saying, "John's doing this and he's doing that," and "John's crazy." I was always the one that must be crazy because I wouldn't let him have status quo. And I came up [*to Yoko*]—was it my idea or yours? Well, we came up with the idea to give it all away and stop fucking about with a psychedelic clothes shop. So we gave it all away.

---

[21] Clive Epstein, Brian's brother, worked with the financial administration of NEMS Enterprises, the Beatles' management company.

[22] The Fool was a fashion designer who designed and manufactured clothing for Apple.

Were you there for the giveaway?

No, we read it in the paper. That was when we started events. I learned events from Yoko. We made everything into an event from then on.

When you gave away your MBE[23] . . .

Yeah. Yeah. I'd been planning on it for over a year and a bit. I was waiting for the time to do it.

You said then that you were waiting to tag it to some event, and then you realized that it was an event in itself.

Yeah. Yeah. That's the truth.

You also said at that time that you had another thing you were going to do.

I don't know what it was.

Do you remember?

Yeah, I do. We always kept them on their toes during our events period. We said, "Well we got some other surprise for them later." I can't remember what it was. Maybe we were getting married. No, we were married. I don't know.

YOKO: You mean after the baby died.[24]

JOHN: After the MBE, we probably intimated that we had another surprise event coming up shortly.

YOKO: Well, probably that was "War Is Over."

JOHN: Probably the "War Is Over" poster event, maybe.

---

[23] "Member of the British Empire" medal awarded to each of the Beatles by the Queen of England in October 1965.

[24] Yoko Ono miscarried with the couple's first child in November 1968.

To go back to Apple and the breakup of the Beatles, Brian died . . .

I didn't really want to do all this. Go on.

You don't?

Well, we're halfway through it now, so let's do it.

You said you quit the Beatles first. How?

Well, I said to Paul, "I'm leaving." We were in Apple and I knew before I went to Toronto, I told Allen I was leaving.[25] I told Eric Clapton and Klaus that I was leaving and I'd like to probably use them as a group.[26] I hadn't decided how to do it, to have a permanent new group or what. And then later on I thought, "Fuck it, I'm not going to get stuck with another set of people, whoever they are." So I announced it to myself and to the people around me on the way to Toronto the few days before. On the plane Allen came with me, and I told him, "It's over." When I got back [to London], there were a few meetings and Allen said, "Cool it," cause there was a lot to do [with the Beatles] business-wise, and it wouldn't have been suitable at the time [to announce my departure]. Then we were discussing something in the office with Paul and Paul was saying to do something, and I kept saying, "No, no, no" to everything he said. So it came to a point that I had to say something. So I said, "The group's over, I'm leaving." Allen was there, and he was saying, "Don't tell." He didn't want me to tell Paul even. But I couldn't help it, I couldn't stop it, it came out. And Paul

---

[25] Allen Klein had been the business manager for the Rolling Stones and had become the manager of John, George and Ringo after Brian Epstein died.

[26] Klaus Voormann was a bassist and artist whom the Beatles first met in Hamburg before they became famous. He later designed the *Revolver* album cover.

and Allen said they were glad that I wasn't going to announce it, like I was going to make an event out of it. I don't know whether Paul said, "Don't tell anybody," but he was damn pleased that I wasn't. He said, "Oh well, that means nothing really happened if you're not going to say anything." So that's what happened.

How did Paul react when you said you were quitting?

Well, like when you say "divorce," the face goes all sorts of colors. It's like he knew *really* that this was the final thing. And then six months later Paul comes out with whatever [his announcement of leaving the band for a solo career]. A lot of people knew I'd left, but I was a fool not to do what Paul did, which is use it to sell a record.

You were really angry with Paul.

No, I wasn't angry.

Well, when he came out with his "I'm leaving."

I wasn't angry, I was just— "shit!" He's a good PR man, Paul. I mean he's about the best in the world, probably. He really does a job. I wasn't angry. We were all hurt that he didn't tell us what he was going to do. I think he claims that he didn't mean that to happen, but that's bullshit. He called me in the afternoon of that day and said, "I'm doing what you and Yoko were doing."

YOKO: Last year.

JOHN: Last year. And I said, "Good." Because that time last year, they were all looking at us as if it was strange trying to make a life together and doing all the things and being fab, fat myths. So he rang me up on that day and said, "I'm doing what you and Yoko are doing and putting out an album. And *I'm* leaving the group too," he said. I said "Good." I was feeling a little strange, because *he* was saying it this time—a year later. I said "good," cause he was the one that wanted the

Beatles most. And then the midnight papers came out [announcing Paul had left the band].

How did you feel then?

I was cursing because I hadn't done it.

YOKO: [*Laugh*] He sold a record [*McCartney*] that virtually didn't have any message in it . . .

JOHN: Well, you don't have to have a message in a record. But he just did a great hype. I wanted to do it and I should have done it. I think, Damn, shit, what a fool I was. But there were many pressures at that time with [the Beatles' publisher] Northern Songs and all that was going, and it would have upset the whole thing if I'd have said that.

How did you feel when you found out that Dick James had sold his shares in Northern Songs?[27]

I was pissed off.

Did you feel betrayed?

Sure I do, you know. I mean he's another one of them people, a bit like George Martin, who think they made us. And they didn't. I'd like to hear Dick James's music, I'd like to hear George Martin's music please, just play me some. And Dick James actually has said that . . .

What?

That he made us. People are under a delusion that they made us.

How did Dick James tell you about the sale?

He didn't tell us. He *did* it. It was just a *fait accompli*. He went and sold to Lew Grade, that's all we knew. We read it in the paper, I think.

---

[27] Dick James was a London music publisher who established Northern Songs with Brian Epstein. James had 55 percent ownership of Northern Songs.

What was that part about Lew Grade?[28]

It was fantastic. It was like this room full of old men smoking and fighting. People seem to think businessmen like Allen or Grade or any of them are a race apart. They play the game the way we play music, and it's something to see. They have ritual and they create—like Allen is a very creative guy. He creates situations which create positions for them to move in. They all do it. It was a sight to see. We played our part, we both did.

What did you do?

With the bankers and things like that. Allen will tell you better because you can't say anything about anybody cause you get sued or something. So check Allen with that, he'll tell you what we did. I did a job on this banker that we were all using. And a few other people. And on the Beatles.

What kind of "job"?

Well how do you describe the job? I maneuver people. That's what leaders do. I sit and make situations in which it's a benefit to me with other people. It's as simple as that.

YOKO: Oh, I think we should cut that out.

JOHN: Why?

YOKO: That's the way you always feel, but afterward you can never . . .

JOHN: I maneuvered too. I had to do a job to get Allen in Apple.

YOKO: Exactly.

JOHN: I did a job. So did Yoko.

YOKO: You do it—you do it with instinct, not by cunning . . .

---

[28] Sir Lew Grade's entertainment company ATV bought Northern Songs in 1969.

JOHN: Oh, God, Yoko, don't say that. *Maneuvering* is what it is, let's not be coy about it. It's a deliberate and thought-out maneuver of how to get a situation how we *want* it. That's how life's about, isn't it? Is it not? Is it?

YOKO: Well, you're a pretty instinctive guy—

JOHN: So is Allen, so is Dick James, so is Grade, they're all instinctive. So is he [Jann], I mean it's instinctive, but it's maneuvering. There's nothing ashamed about it, we *all* do it, it's just owning up, not going around saying, "God bless you brother, Hare fucking Krishna," and doing it, pretending there's no interest.

YOKO: No, the difference is that you don't go to Allen and bullshit and get him. You just instinctively suss [out] that Allen is the guy—you jump into it and you just get him.

JOHN: But that's not the point. What I'm talking about is creating a situation around Apple and the Beatles in which Allen could come in. He wouldn't have got in unless I'd done it—

YOKO: Right. That's true.

JOHN: —and he wouldn't have got in unless you'd done it. You made the decision too.

How did you get Allen?

The same as I get anything I want—the same as you get what you want. I'm not telling you.

Just work at it hard.

Just work at it and get on the phone and a little word here and a little word there and do it.

What was Paul's reaction?

See, a lot of people—Dick James and the Derek Taylors and Peter Brown, all of them, you know, they think they're the Beatles and

▸

Neil[29] and all of them. Well I say, fuck 'em. After working with genius for ten, fifteen years, they begin to think they're it. They're *not*.

Do you think you're a genius?

Yes. If there's such a thing as one, I *am* one.

When did you first realize it?

When I was about twelve. I used to think, I must be a genius, but nobody's noticed [*laugh*]. Either I'm a genius or I'm mad, which is it? "No," I said, "I can't be mad because nobody's put me away; therefore, I'm a genius." Genius is a form of madness and we're all that way. But I used to be a bit coy about it, like me guitar playing. If there's such a thing as genius—which is just *what*? What the fuck is it—I am one. And if there isn't, I don't care. But I used to think, when I was a kid, writing me poetry and doing me paintings—I didn't become something when the Beatles made it or when you heard about me, I've been like this all me life. Genius is *pain* too. It's just pain.

How do you feel toward Apple? You talk about Mal[30] and Derek . . .

I didn't mention Mal. I said Neil, Peter Brown and Derek. They live in a dream of Beatle past and everything they do is oriented to that. They also have a warped view of what was happening.

They must feel now that their lives are just inextricably bound up in yours.

Well, they have to grow up then—because they've only had half their life. They've got another whole half to go and they can't go on

---

[29] Neil Aspinall was hired as the Beatles' road manager in 1961 and later was the head of Apple Corps.

[30] Mal Evans was the Beatles' roadie and bodyguard.

pretending to be Beatles. That's where it's at. They don't know. When they read it, they'll think, "It's cracked John," if it's in the article. But that's where it's at. They live in the past.

You traveled to Toronto with Derek, right? And also did a Bed Peace up there.

That was the same thing, yeah. Well, I was living in the past too then. See, I presumed I would just be able to carry on and just bring Yoko into our life, but it seemed that I either had to be married to them or Yoko. I chose Yoko. You know? And I was right.

How did you meet Yoko?

I'm sure I've told you this many times. How did I meet Yoko? There was a sort of underground clique in London: John Dunbar, who was married to Marianne Faithfull, had an art gallery in London called Indica and I'd been going around to galleries a bit on my off days in between records. I'd been to see a Takis exhibition—I don't know if you know what that means—he does multiple electro-magnetic sculptures, and a few exhibitions in different galleries who showed these sort of unknown artists or underground artists. I got the word that this amazing woman was putting on a show next week and there was going to be something about people in bags, in black bags, and it was going to be a bit of a happening and all that. So I went down to a preview of the show. I got there the night before it opened. I went in—she didn't know who I was or anything—I was wandering around, there was a couple of artsy type students that had been help-ing lying around there in the gallery, and I was looking at it and I was astounded. There was an apple on sale there for two hundred quid, I thought it was fantastic—I got the humor in her work immediately. I didn't have to have much knowledge about avant-garde or underground art, but the humor got me straightaway. There was a fresh apple on a stand—this was before Apple—and it was two hundred quid to watch the apple decompose. But there was another piece which really decided me for-or-against the artist: a ladder which led to a painting which was hung on the ceiling. It looked like a black canvas with a chain with a spyglass hanging on the end of it. This was near the door when you went in. I climbed the ladder, you look through the spyglass and in tiny little letters it says "yes." So it was positive. I felt relieved. It's a great relief when you get up the ladder and you look through the spyglass and it doesn't say "no" or "fuck you" or something, it said "yes."

I was very impressed and John Dunbar introduced us—neither of us knew who the hell we were, she didn't know who I was, she'd only heard of Ringo, I think, it means apple in Japanese. And John Dunbar had been sort of hustling her saying, "That's a good patron, you must go and talk to him or do something," because I was looking for action, I was expecting a happening and things like that. John Dunbar insisted she say hello to the millionaire. And she came up and handed me a card which said "breathe" on it, one of her instructions, so I just went [pant]. This was our meeting.

Then I went away, and the second time I met her at a gallery opening of Claes Oldenburg in London. We were very shy, we nodded at each other and we didn't know—she was standing behind me, I looked away because I'm very shy with people, especially chicks. We just smiled and stood frozen together in this cocktail party thing.

The next thing was she came to me to get some backing—like all the bastard underground do—for a show she was doing. She gave me her *Grapefruit* book and I used to read it and sometimes I'd get very annoyed by it; it would say things like "paint until you drop dead" or "bleed" and then sometimes I'd be very enlightened by it and I went through all the changes that people go through with her work—sometimes I'd have it by the bed and I'd open it and it would say something nice and it would be alright and then it would say something heavy and I wouldn't like it. There was all that, and then she came to me to get some backing for a show and it was half a wind show. I gave her the money to back it and the show was—this was in a place called Lisson Gallery, another one of those underground places. For this whole show everything was in half: There was half a bed, half a room, half of everything, all beautifully cut in half and all painted white. And I said to her, "Why don't you sell the other half in bottles?" having caught on by then what the game was and she did that—this is still before we'd had any nuptials—and we still have the bottles from the show, it's my first. It was presented as "Yoko Plus Me"—that was our first public appearance. I didn't even go to see the show, I was too uptight.

When did you realize that you were in love with her?

It was beginning to happen; I would start looking at her book and that, but I wasn't quite aware what was happening to me, and then she did a thing called Dance Event, where different cards kept coming through the door every day saying "Breathe" and "Dance" and "Watch all the lights until dawn," and they upset me or made me happy depending on how I felt.

I'd get very upset about it being intellectual or all fucking avant garde, then I'd like it and then I wouldn't. Then I went to India with the

Maharishi and we were corresponding. The letters were still formal, but they just had a little side to them. I nearly took her to India as I said, but I still wasn't sure for what reason, I was still sort of kidding myself, with sort of artistic reasons, and all that.

When we got back from India, we were talking to each other on the phone. I called her over, it was the middle of the night and Cyn was away, and I thought, "Well, now's the time if I'm gonna get to know her anymore." She came to the house and I didn't know what to do; so we went upstairs to my studio and I played her all the tapes that I'd made, all this far-out stuff, some comedy stuff, and some electronic music. There were very few people I could play those tapes to. She was suitably impressed, and then she said, "Well, let's make one ourselves," so we made *Two Virgins*.[31] It was midnight when we started *Two Virgins*, it was dawn when we finished, and then we made love at dawn. It was very beautiful.

What was Cynthia like then?

I don't remember. She was away on holiday, both our respective spouses were on holiday when we got together. And that was it. I don't know. I didn't communicate with her.

What was your and Yoko's wedding like? Did you enjoy it?

It was very romantic. It's all in the song, "The Ballad of John and Yoko." If you want to know how it happened, it's in there. Gibraltar was like a little sunny dream. I couldn't find a white suit—I had off-white corduroy trousers and a white jacket. Yoko had all white on.

What was your first peace event?

[31] John and Yoko's first album together, *Unfinished Music No. 1: Two Virgins*, was released by Apple in 1968..

The first peace event was the Amsterdam Bed Peace when we got married.

What was that like? That was your first re-exposure to the public.

It was a nice high. We were on the seventh floor of the Hilton looking over Amsterdam. It was very crazy, the press came expecting to see us fucking in bed—they all heard John and Yoko were going to fuck in front of the press for peace. So when they all walked in—about fifty or sixty reporters flew over from London all sort of very edgy, and we were just sitting in pajamas saying, "Peace, brother" and that was it. On the peace thing there's lots of heavy discussion with intellectuals about how you should do it and how you shouldn't.

When you got alone, did you feel satisfied with the Bed Peace . . .?

That was beautiful. It was like the wedding album, and it was a move for peace. I mean it's no question about it. They were great events when you think that the world newspaper headlines were the fact that we were a married couple in bed talking about peace. It was one of our greater episodes. It was like being on tour without moving, sort of a big promotional thing. I think we did a good job for what we were doing, which was trying to get people to own up.

You chose the word "peace" and not "love," or another word that means the same thing. What did you like about the word "peace"?

Yoko and I were discussing our different lives and careers when we first got together. What we had in common in a way, was that she'd done things for peace like standing in Trafalgar Square in a black bag and things like that—we were just trying to work out what we could do—and the Beatles had been singing about "love" and things. So we pooled our resources and came out with the Bed Peace—it was some way of doing something together that wouldn't involve me standing in Trafalgar Square in a black bag because I was too nervous to do that. Yoko didn't want to do anything that wasn't for peace.

Did you ever get any reaction from political leaders?

I don't know about the Bed-In. We got reaction to sending acorns—different heads of state actually planted their acorns, lots of them wrote to us answering about the acorns. We sent acorns to practically everybody in the world.

Who answered?

Well, I believe Golda Meir said, "I don't know who they are but if it's for peace, we're for it" or something like that. Scandinavia, somebody or other planted it. I think Haile Selassie planted his, I'm not sure. Some queen somewhere. There was quite a few people that understood the idea.

Did you send one to Queen Elizabeth?

We sent one to Harold Wilson, I don't think we got a reply from Harold, did we?

What was it like meeting [Canadian] Prime Minister Trudeau? What was his response to you?

He was interested in us because he thought we might represent some sort of youth faction—he wants to know, like everybody does, really. I think he was very nervous—he was more nervous than we were when we met. We talked about everything—just anything you can think of. We spent about forty minutes—it was five minutes longer than he'd spent with heads of state, which was the great glory of the time. He'd read *In His Own Write*, my book, and things like that. He liked the poetry side of it. We just wanted to see what they did, how they worked.

You appeared in the bags for Hanratty.[32]

For Hanratty, yes, we did a sort of bag event, but it wasn't us in the bag, it was somebody else. The best thing we did in a bag together was a press conference in Vienna. When they were showing Yoko's [film] *Rape* on Austrian TV—they commissioned us to make the film and then we went over to Vienna to see it.

It was like a hotel press conference. We kept them out of the room. We came down the elevator in the bag and we went in and we got comfortable and they were all ushered in. It was a very strange scene because they'd never seen us before, or heard—Vienna is a pretty square place. A few people were saying "C'mon, get out of the bags." And we wouldn't let 'em see us. They all stood back saying. "Is it really John and Yoko?" and "What are you wearing and why are you doing this?" We said, "This is total communication with no prejudice." It was just great. They asked us to sing and we sang a few numbers. Yoko was singing a Japanese folk song, very nicely, just very straight we did it. And they never did see us.

What kind of response did you get to the "War Is Over" poster?[33]

We got a big response. The people that got in touch with us understood what a grand event it was apart from the message itself. We got just thank yous from lots of youths around the world—for all the

---

[32] In April 1962, James Hanratty was hanged for murder and a sex crime in England. John Lennon and Yoko Ono supported Hanratty's family in their ongoing fight to prove his innocence.

[33] In December 1969, John and Yoko launched a billboard campaign in twelve cities around the world. The signs read "War Is Over!/If You Want It/Happy Christmas from John & Yoko."

things we were doing—that inspired *them* to do something. We had a lot of response from other than pop fans, which was interesting, from all walks of life and age. If I walk down the street now I'm more liable to get talked to about peace than anything I've done. The first thing that happened in New York was just walking down the street and a woman just came to me and said, "Good luck with the peace thing." That's what goes on mainly—it's not about "I Want to Hold Your Hand." And that was interesting—it bridged a lot of gaps.

What were the Beatles' reactions when you first brought Yoko by?

They despised her.

From the very beginning?

They insulted her and they still do. Yeah, they don't even know I can see it. And even when it's written down, it'll look like I'm just paranoid or she's paranoid. But I know just by the way the publicity on us was handled by Apple, all of the two years we were together, and the attitude of people to us and the bits we hear from the office girls. So they can go stuff themselves.

YOKO: In the beginning we were too much in love to notice anything else.

JOHN: Yeah. We were in our own dream. They're the kind of idiots that really think that Yoko split the Beatles, or Allen, it's the same joke. They're that insane about Allen, too.

How would you characterize George, Paul and Ringo's reaction to her?

It's the same. You can quote Paul, you can look it up in the papers. He's said many times, at first he hated Yoko and then he got to like her. It's too late for me. And for Yoko. Why should she take that kind of shit from those people? They're writing about her looking miserable in *Let It Be*. You sit through sixty sessions with the most big-headed, uptight people on earth and see what it's fuckin' like. And be insulted just because you love someone. George insulted her right to her face in the Apple office at the beginning, just being straightforward, that game of, "Well, I'm going to be upfront because this is what I've heard and Dylan and a few people said you've got a lousy name in New York and you give off bad vibes." That's what George said to her, and we both sat through it. And I didn't hit him, I don't know why. But I was always hoping that they'd come round. I couldn't believe it! They all sat there with their wives like a fucking jury and judged us. The only thing I did was write that piece about "some of our beast friends"—in my usual way, cause I was never honest. I always had to write in that gobbledy-gook. And that's what they did to us. Ringo was alright. So was Maureen.[34]

But the other two really gave it to us. I'll never forgive them. I don't care what fuckin' shit about Hare Krishna and God and Paul—well, I've changed me mind. I don't forgive 'em for that.

Some people said that when Paul's album came out with a baby on the cover that it was done as a deliberate insult to you and Yoko because you'd lost your baby . . .

No, I don't think he did that. I think he was just imitating us as they usually do, by putting out a family album. You watch—they do exactly what I do a year or two later. [*To Yoko*] This [article] is gonna be some fuckin' thing—it's the end of it. They're imitators, you know.

What do you think people will do with your new album, in terms of imitating it?

[34] Ringo's then-wife, Maureen Cox Starkey.

Well I've [got] no idea.

YOKO: It's a *fantastic* strong album. So one way or other, people are going to either hate it or love it passionately . . .

JOHN: I personally will probably come out next with "wop-bop-aloo-bop" or something. I mean, I've said it for a bit.

YOKO: You've said it enough for ten years . . .

When did you realize that you were just not going to be able to reconcile Paul and George to Yoko?

I don't know when it was—when I decided to leave the group.

Did Yoko's avant-garde music background clash with the music the Beatles made?

Yoko played me tapes that I understood. I know it was very strange, and avant-garde music is a tough thing to assimilate and all that. But I've heard the Beatles playing avant-garde music when nobody was looking for years. But they're artists, and all artists have fuckin' big egos. Whether they like to admit it or not. And when a new artist came into the group, they were never allowed. Sometimes George and I would like to bring someone in, like Billy Preston. We would have had him in the group. We were fed up with the same old shit. But it wasn't wanted. I would have expanded the Beatles, gotten their pants off, stopped being God. But it didn't work.

YOKO: It's very difficult.

JOHN: It didn't work and Yoko was naïve, she came in and would expect to perform with them, like you would with any group. She was jammin'. But they'd [have] a sort of coldness about it. When I decided to leave the group, I decided that I could no longer artistically get anything out of the Beatles. And here was somebody that could turn me on to a million things.

How did you choose the musicians you use on this album?

I'm a very nervous person, really. I'm not as big-headed as this tape sounds. This is me projecting through the fear. So I chose people that I know rather than strangers.

Like you used Ringo. Why do you get along with Ringo?

Because in spite of all the things . . . the Beatles really could play music together when they weren't uptight. And if I get a thing going, Ringo knows where to go. Like *that.* We've played together so long that it fits. That's the only thing I sometimes miss is, is being able to just sort of blink or make a certain noise and I know they'll all know where we're going on an ad lib thing. But I don't miss it *that* much.

You always said the Beatles wanted to be bigger than Elvis. Why?

Because Elvis was the biggest. We wanted to be the biggest. Doesn't everybody?

When did you decide that?

Well, first of all, Paul and I wanted to be the Goffin and King of England.[35] This is an old story. Because Goffin and King were writing this great stuff at that time. And then we decided, well, we're better than them, so we want to be this, we want to be the next thing, we want to be president or whatever. It goes on and on and on. But we always wanted to be bigger than Elvis, cause Elvis was *the* thing. Whatever we say, he was *it.*

At what moment did you realize that you were bigger than Elvis?

---

[35] Gerry Goffin and Carole King were the songwriting duo responsible for numerous hit singles beginning in the early Sixties. King would become a very successful singer/songwriter in the Seventies.

I don't know. It's different when it happens, you've forgotten about [your desire for] it. It's like when you actually get the Number One or whatever it is, it's different. It's the going for it which is the fun.

So at some point you just never thought about it again.

Yeah, yeah, we were just like jelly, we sat in a mold and we floated about like that.

In "God," you say, "the dream is over" and part of the dream was "the Beatles were God" . . .

Yeah, if there *is* a God, we're all *it*.

When did you first start getting the spiritual reactions from people who had listened to Beatles records?

There's a guy in England called William Mann who writes in *The Times* who wrote the first intellectual review of the Beatles, which got people talking about us in that intellectual way. He wrote about Aeolian cadences and all sort of musical terms. He's a bullshitter, but he wrote about Paul's album as if it was written by Beethoven, this last one. He's just voted it the album of the year and all that shit. He's still writing the same shit. But it did us a lot of good in that way, cause people—all the middle classes and intellectuals—are going, "Ooh, aren't they clever."

YOKO: When did they start the message thing?

JOHN: The message thing? About love and that?

When did somebody first come up to you with "John Lennon is God"?

"What to do" and all that? Like, "You tell us, guru." That bit?

Yeah.

Probably after acid. *Rubber Soul?* Well, I don't know, I can't quite remember. I can't remember it exactly happening. We just took that position. I mean we started putting out messages—like "the word" and "the word is love" and things like that. I like messages.

YOKO: Well, "Strawberry Fields" is a message . . .

JOHN: That's later on, this is earlier on, you see. When you start putting out messages, people start coming and asking you, "What's the message?"

How did you first get involved with LSD?

A dentist in London.

YOKO: [*laugh*] A dentist.

JOHN: He laid it on George, me and our wives without telling us at a dinner party at his house. He was a friend of George's, and our dentist at the time. He just put it in our coffee or something. He didn't know what it was, it was just, "It's all the thing," with the middle-class London swingers. They had all heard about it and didn't know it was different from pot or pills. And they gave it to us, and he was saying, "I advise you not to leave," and we thought he was trying to keep us for an orgy in his house and we didn't want to *know*. We went out to the Ad Lib [nightclub] and these discotheques and there was incredible things going on. This guy came with us, he was nervous, he didn't know what was going on. We were going crackers. It was insane going around London on it. When we entered the club, we thought it was on fire. And then we thought it was a premiere, but it was just an ordinary light outside. We thought, "Shit, what's going on here?" And we were cackling in the street, and then people were shouting, "Let's break a window." We were just *insane*. We were just out of our heads. We finally got in the lift and we all thought there was a fire in the lift. It was just a little red light, and we were all *screaming*—it was hysterical. We all arrived on the floor, cause this was a discotheque that was up a building. The lift stops and the door opens and we're all going, "*Aaahhhhh*" [*loud scream*], and we just see that it's the club, and then we walk in, sit down, and the table's elongating. I think we went to eat before that, where the table went *this* long, just like I'd read somebody—who is it, Blake, is it?—somebody describing the effects of the opium in the old days. And I thought, "Fuck, it's happening." And then we went to the Ad Lib and all that. And then some singer came up to me and said, "Can I sit next to you?" And I was going, [*loudly*], "*Only if you don't talk*," [*laugh*], cause I just couldn't think.

When you came down, what did you think?

I was pretty stunned for a month or two.

Where did you go after that?   ·

It seemed to go on all night. I can't remember the details, it just went on like that. And then George somehow or another managed to drive us home in his mini. We were going about ten miles an hour, but it seemed like a thousand. And Pattie was saying, "Let's jump out and play football, there's these big rugby poles" and things like that.[36] I was getting all this sort of hysterical jokes coming out, like with speed, because I was always on that, too.

George was going, "*Don't make me laugh!*" Oh God! It was just terrifying. But it was fantastic. I did some drawings at the time—I've got them somewhere—of four faces and "we all agree with you," things like that. I gave them to Ringo, I've lost the originals. I did a lot of drawing that night—[*sound to imitate fast sketching*]—just like that. And then George's house seemed to be just like a big submarine. I was driving it—they all went to bed and I was carrying on on me own—it seemed

---

[36]   Pattie Boyd Harrison, George's then-wife.

to float above his wall, which was eighteen foot, and I was driving it. And the second time, we had [acid] in L.A., which was different.

What happened then?

Well, then we took it deliberately.

To backtrack a second, afterwards everybody slept?

Oh, I don't remember. We were all just a bit down after it. Wow, you know, I don't remember that kind of thing, I only remember the highlights. And then, well, we just decided to take it again in California.

Where were you when you took it the second time?

We were on tour, in one of those houses, like Doris Day's house or wherever it was we used to stay. And the three of us took it. Ringo, George and I. I think, maybe Neil. And a couple of the Byrds, you know, that what's-his-name, the one in the Stills and Nash thing.[37] You know the Byrds? B-Y-R-D—Crosby and the other guy, who used to be the leader.

McGuinn.[38]

McGuinn. I think they came round, I'm not sure, on a few trips. But there were so many reporters, there was like Don Short and that.[39] We were in the garden, it was only the second one. We still didn't know anything about doing it in a nice place and cool it and all that, we just took it. And all of a sudden we saw the reporter and we're thinking, "How do we act normal?" Because we imagined we were acting extraordinary, which we weren't. We thought, "Surely somebody can see." We were

---

[37] Crosby, Stills and Nash had just formed and consisted of ex-Byrd David Crosby, Stephen Stills and Graham Nash.

[38] Roger McGuinn was the founder of the Byrds.

[39] Don Short was a journalist who traveled extensively with the Beatles between 1963 and 1970.

terrified waiting for him to go, and he wondered why he couldn't come over, and Neil, who had never had it either, had taken it, and he still had to play road manager. We said, "Go and get rid of Don Short," and he didn't know what to do, he just sort of sat with it. And Peter Fonda came, that was another thing, and he kept on saying [*whispering*], "I know what it's like to be dead." We said, "What?" And he kept saying it, and we were saying, "For chrissake, shut up, we don't care. We don't want to know." But he kept going on about it.[40] That's how I wrote "She Said She Said." [*half singing*] "I know what it's like to be dead."

What else entered into that song?

Well, it was a sad song. It was just an acid-y song, it was. "And when I was a little boy, he said."[41] Oh, a lot of, early childhood was coming out anyway.

So how long did LSD go on?

It went on for years. I must have had a thousand trips.

Literally a thousand or—

Yeah.

A couple hundred?

No, lots. I used to just eat it all the time. I never took it in the studio. Once I did accidentally. I thought I was taking some uppers, and I was not in a state of handling it. I can't remember what album it was, but I took it and then [*whispers*] I just noticed all of a sudden I got so scared on the mike. I said, "What was it?" I thought I felt ill. I thought I was going cracked. Then I said, "I must get some air." They all took

---

[40] When he was ten, Peter Fonda shot himself, and he has said, "For forty seconds it seemed like I was dying."

[41] Song lyric is "When I was a boy everything was right."

me upstairs on the roof, and George Martin was looking at me funny. And then it dawned on me, I must have taken acid. And I said, "Well, I can't go on, I have to go." So I just said, "You'll have to do it and I'll just stay and watch." I just [became] very nervous and [was] just watching all of a sudden. "Is it alright?" And they were saying, "Yeah." They were all being very kind. They said, "Yes, it's alright." And I said, "Are you sure it's alright?" They carried on making the record.

The other Beatles didn't get into LSD as much as you did.

George did . . . in L.A. Paul felt very out of it cause we were all a bit cruel. It's like, "We're taking it and you're not." We couldn't eat our food, I just couldn't manage it. Picking it up with the hands, and there's all these people serving us in the house, and we're just knocking it on the floor—oh!—like that. It was a long time before Paul took it. And then there was the big announcement.[42] I think George was pretty heavy on it. We were probably both the most cracked. I think Paul's a bit more stable than George and I.

He's more straight . . .

I don't know about straight. Stable. I think LSD profoundly shocked him.

Did you ever start getting bad trips?

Oh yeah, I had many. Jesus Christ. I stopped taking it cause of that. I mean I just—

YOKO: Couldn't stand it.

JOHN: —couldn't stand it. I dropped it for I don't know how long. Then I started taking it just before I met Yoko. I got a message on acid that you should destroy your ego, and I did. I was reading that stupid

[42] In 1967, Paul publicly admitted taking LSD.

book of Leary's and all that shit.[43] We were going through a whole game that everybody went through. And I destroyed meself. I was slowly putting meself together after Maharishi, bit by bit, over a two-year period. And then I destroyed me ego and I didn't believe I could do *anything*. I let Paul do what he wanted and say, them all just do what they wanted. And I just was nothing, I was *shit*. And then Derek [Taylor] tripped me out at his house after he'd got back from L.A. He said, "You're alright." And he pointed out which songs I'd written, and said, "You wrote this, and you said this, and you are intelligent, don't be frightened." The next week I went down with Yoko and we tripped out again, and she freed me completely, to realize that I was *me* and it's alright. And that was it. I started fighting again and being a loud-mouth again and saying, "Well, I can do this," and "Fuck you, and this is what *I* want," and "Don't put me down. I did *this*." So that's where I am now.

There's a lot of obvious references to LSD in your music. "Tomorrow Never Knows" . . .

Yeah.

How do you think acid affected your conception of music in general?

Well, it was only another mirror—it wasn't another miracle. It was more of a visual thing, and the therapy, that "looking at yourself" bit, it did all that. I don't quite remember. You hear the music, but *it* didn't *write* the music, neither did Janov or Maharishi on the same terms . . .

---

[43] Published in 1964, *The Psychedelic Experience* was written by Timothy Leary in collaboration with Ralph Metzer and Richard Alpert, and was intended as a manual for using LSD. Its instructions included the recitation of such concepts as "that which is called ego death is coming to you."

I write the music in the circumstances in which I'm in, whether it's on acid or in the water.

YOKO: And in all those trips you just didn't lose yourself.

"She Said She Said" was the first song you wrote that had something connected with it, an influential drug experience?

No, not really. There's nothing I can pinpoint. *Rubber Soul* was pot, or the one before with the drawing on it [*Revolver*]. Pills influenced [the music] in Hamburg, and drink influenced us and so and so. There's no specific things. I only wrote ["She Said She Said"] cause the guy said, "I know what it's like to be dead." If I'd read it in the paper, I would have written a song about it. And to write a mood song—if I'm sad, I would just write sort of sad things, just remember sad things. "When I was a boy, everything was right" and all that, which is a dream. I would put myself in a sad mood and write a sad song. Or be in a sad mood and write a song, is more like it.

What did you think when you saw 'Hard Day's Night'?

I thought it wasn't bad. It could have been better. There's another illusion that we were just puppets and that these great people like Brian Epstein and Dick Lester created this situation and made this whole fuckin' thing, precisely because we were what we were and realistic.[44] We didn't want to make a fuckin' shitty pop movie. We didn't even want to make a movie that was going to be bad. And we insisted on having a

---

[44] Richard Lester directed the Beatles films *A Hard Day's Night* and *Help!*, as well as the film *How I Won the War*, in which John Lennon had an acting role.

real writer and Brian came up with Alun Owen, from Liverpool, who'd written a play for TV called *No Trams to Lime Street*, which I knew and maybe they all knew. Lime Street's a famous street in Liverpool where the whores used to be in the old days. And he was famous for writing Liverpool dialogue. We auditioned people to write for us. They came up with this guy, and we knew his work, and we said, "Alright." But then he had to come round with us to see what we were like. He was a *phony*— like a professional Liverpool man, or like professional Americans, like that. And he stayed with us two days and wrote the whole thing based on our characters: me, witty; Ringo, dumb, cute; George, this; Paul, that. We were a bit infuriated by the glibness of it, and the shittiness of the dialogue. We were always trying to get it more realistic, even with Dick [Lester] and all that, and make the camera work more realistic. But they wouldn't have it. They made *that* movie and so that's how it happened. And the next one was just bullshit. I just hate this illusion about George Martin, Brian Epstein, Dick Lester and all these people making something out of us. *We're* the ones that are still creating.

My impression from the movie was that it was you and it wasn't anybody else.

It was a good projection of one facade of us, which was on tour, once in London and once in Dublin. Of us in that situation together. In a hotel having to perform before people. We were like that. Alun Owen saw the press conferences. He recreated it pretty well, but we thought it was phony then even. It wasn't realistic enough.

Were you aware of the impact that 'Hard Day's Night' had in the States? I mean other than being tremendously popular?

I don't remember. All we knew was "big hit or no hit." If it was a big hit or not.

You see, 'Hard Day's Night' was sort of the period when the Byrds started, and all the American musicians went and saw 'Hard Day's Night' and realized rock & roll was okay.

I see. I see. No, I wasn't ever aware of those impacts. I was aware of musical impacts more, listening to—"I know he got that from us and we got that from [him]"—that kind of thing.

What had you heard?

Oh, I don't know, I can just tell where the groups came from, any of them now I can tell—like [Led] Zeppelin and Fleetwood Mac, you can hear where everything came from. Same as you can with anybody.

I remember this single coming out, "Day Tripper/We Can Work It Out."

Yeah, that was a drug song.

"Day Tripper"?

Um.

Why?

Cause it was a day tripper. I just liked the word.

At some point, right in there between 'Help!' and 'Hard Day's Night,' you got into drugs?

Yeah, but in *Hard Day's Night*, I was on pills. That's drugs, you know, that's bigger drugs than pot. I've been on pills since I was fifteen—no, since I was seventeen. Since I became a musician. The only way to survive in Hamburg, to play eight hours a night, was to take pills. The waiters gave you the pills and drink. I was fuckin' dropdown drunk in art school. I was a pill addict until *Help!*, just before *Help!* where we were turned onto pot and we dropped drink. Simple as that. I've always needed a drug to *survive*. The others too, but I always had *more*, I always took *more* pills and *more* of everything, cause I'm *more* crazy.

With "Day Tripper," is that when you first started writing message songs? Serious songs?

Probably after Dylan. I don't know. "Day Tripper" wasn't a serious message song, was it?

I don't mean a serious message song in that sense. I mean there was a big change in your music from "Can't Buy Me Love" to "We Can Work It Out," 'Rubber Soul.'

I suppose it was pot then. I don't really know. I can't . . . "We Can Work It Out" Paul wrote that chorus, and I wrote the middle bit about, "Life is very short and there's no time for fussin' and fightin'," all that bit. I don't remember any changeover, other than when you take pot you're a little less aggressive than when you take alcohol. When you're [on] alcohol and pills—it's not anything.

Alright, then let's say 'Rubber Soul' . . .

Can you tell me if that white album[45] with the drawing by Klaus Voormann on it, was that before *Rubber Soul* or after?

After.

Oh, I see, okay, *Rubber Soul* is the one then.

You really don't remember which . . .

No.

Hmmm . . .

Maybe the others do. I don't remember those kind of things, because it doesn't mean anything, it's all gone.

Well 'Rubber Soul' seemed like the first attempt at serious . . .

No, we just were getting better technically and musically, that's all. We finally took over the studio. In the early days we had to take what

[45]   *Revolver*, 1966.

we were given. We had to make it in two hours or whatever it was. And three takes was enough, and we didn't know about "you can get more bass," and we were learning the technique. With *Rubber Soul*, we were more precise about making the album—that's all. We took over the cover and everything.

What was "Rubber Soul"? That was just a simple play on . . .

Oh, that was Paul's title, it was like "Yer Blues," I suppose, meaning English soul. "Rubber Soul" is just a pun. There's no great mysterious meanings behind all of this. It was just four boys working out what to call their new album.

Shall we stop for a while?

I don't mind. No, we better go on, because Yoko's got your pal, Jonathan Cott,[46] to do the same trick with next, how she formed the Beatles in 1929 [*laugh*]. And we like to be together, cause it's nicer.

Why can't you be alone without Yoko?

I can be, but I don't wish to be. There is no reason on earth why I should be without her. There is nothing more important than our relationship, nothing. And we dig being together all the time. And both of us could survive apart, but what for? I'm not going to sacrifice love, real love, for any fuckin' whore or any friend, or any business, because in the end you're alone at night. Neither of us want to be and you can't fill the bed with groupies, that doesn't work. I don't want to be a swinger. Like I said in the song, I've been through it all and nothing works better than to have somebody you love hold you.

---

[46] A ROLLING STONE contributing editor since the magazine's inception in 1967.

There was a while in which you hid out in Weybridge where you sat home all the time and did nothing . . .

Well, that's what they say, but I wrote a lot of songs and made some what would be termed "far out" tapes, which I still have. And I made a lot of movies on 8mm. But at the time I used to think that was not doing anything; I thought if I wasn't doing Beatle work, it wasn't work.

You said at one point you have to write songs that can justify your existence.

I said a lot of things. I write songs because that's the thing I choose to do, and I can't help writing them, that's a fact. And sometimes I feel as though you work—I felt as though you worked to justify your existence, but you don't. You work to exist and vice versa, and that's it, really.

You say you write songs because you can't help it.

Yeah, creating is a result of pain, too. I have to put it somewhere and I write songs. But that hiding in Weybridge, I used to think I wasn't working there. I made twenty or thirty movies, on just 8mm stuff, but they are still movies. And many, many hours of tape of different sounds, just not rocking, I suppose you would call them avant garde.

Why did Derek [Taylor] and Brian [Epstein] fall out?

Because Derek is another egomaniac and Brian was very hard to live with, to take. He had a lot of tantrums and things like that. Like most fags do. They're very insecure. Something happened, which I don't remember, maybe Paul or somebody [would], but you'd have to ask them. They had many arguments and Derek would walk off cause he was too proud to do certain jobs. It's the same now. And I don't blame him, but don't get paid for it. Heh-heh. So that's what happened, they had a big row, and Derek was hired by Brian, so was Peter Brown. They really were not hired by us. We hired Neil in Liverpool and Mal in Liverpool. Those were the only people we ever hired.

The Hunter Davies book says that[47] . . .

Well, it was really bullshit. It was written in the sort of *Sunday Times* [style], "the Fab Four." No truth was written, and my auntie knocked all the truth bits about my childhood and me mother and I allowed her, which is my cop-out, etc. etc. There was nothing about the orgies and the shit that happened on tour and all that. And I wanted a *real* book to come out, but we all had wives and didn't want to hurt their feelings. End of that one, cause they still have. You know, I mean the Beatles' tours were like Fellini's *Satyricon*.

YOKO: [*laugh*]

JOHN: We had that image, but man, our tours were like something else, if you could get on our tours you were *in*. Just think of *Satyricon*, with four musicians going through it.

Would you go to a town, a hotel . . .

Wherever we went, there was always a whole scene going. We had our four bedrooms separate from—tried to keep 'em out of our room, and Derek and Neil's rooms were always full of junk and whores and fuck knows what. And policemen, *everything*. *Satyricon*, you know. We really . . . well, we had to do *something*. And what do you do if the pill doesn't wear off—when it's time to go. You just go. I used to be up all night with Derek, whether there was anybody there or not. I just could never sleep. Such a heavy scene it was. They didn't call them groupies

[47] *The Beatles: The Authorized Biography* (1969).

then, they called it something else. But if we couldn't have groupies, we'd have whores and everything, whatever. Whatever was going.

Who would arrange for all that stuff?

Derek and Neil, that was their job, and Mal, but I'm not going into all that.

It's like businessmen on a convention.

Oh, sure it was. When we hit town, we *hit* it. We're not pissin' about. There's photographs of me crawling about in Amsterdam on me knees, coming out of whorehouses and things like that. And people saying [*cheerily*], "Good morning, John." The police escorting me to the places because they never wanted a big scandal, you see. I don't really want to talk about it, cause it hurt Yoko. And it's not fair. But suffice to say, just put it like, "*They* were *Satyricon* on tour," and that's it. Cause I don't want to hurt the other people's girls either, it's just not fair. I'm sorry.

YOKO: I was surprised! I didn't know things like that. I thought, "Well, John is an artist and probably he had two or three affairs before getting married." That is the concept you have in the old school New York artists' group, you know, that kind.

Generation gap.

YOKO: Right. Right. Exactly [*laugh*].

Certainly George has told Pattie by this time, and . . .

I *don't* think so. I don't think they have. You'd have to ask them . . .

Let me ask you about something else that was in the Hunter Davies book. At one point you and Brian went off to Spain.

Yes.

Did you . . . you must have . . .

We didn't have an affair.

You never had an affair with Brian?

No, not an affair.

YOKO: [*laugh*]

What were the pressures from Brian?

Cyn was having a baby and the holiday was planned, but I wasn't going to break the holiday for a baby and that's what a *bastard* I was.[48] And I just went on holiday. I watched Brian picking up the boys. I like playing a big faggy, all that.

YOKO: [*laugh*]

JOHN: It was enjoyable, but there [were] big rumors in Liverpool, it was terrible. Very embarrassing.

Rumors about you and Brian?

Oh, fuck knows—yes, yes. I was pretty close to Brian because if somebody's going to manage me, I want to know them inside out. And there was a period when he told me he was a fag and all that. I introduced him to pills, which gives me a guilt association for his death. I mean they go that way anyway. And to make him talk—to find out what he's like. And I remember him saying, "Don't ever throw it back in me face, that I'm a fag." Which I didn't. But his mother's still hiding that. But what I hate is the way they're all attacking Allen. And Brian was a nice guy, but he knew what he was doing, he robbed us. He fucking took all the money and looked after himself and his family, and all that. And it's just a myth. I hate the way that Allen is attacked and Brian is made like an angel, just cause he's dead. He *wasn't*, he was just a guy. Allen will go berserk when he hears all this.

What else about that Hunter Davies book?

[48] John's first son, John Charles Julian Lennon, was born on April 8, 1963.

Well, that . . . I don't know, I can't remember it. *Love Me Do* was a better book, by Michael Braun, on the Beatles.[49] That was a true book. He wrote how we were, which was bastards. You can't be anything else in a situation of such pressurized—and we took it out on people like Neil, Derek and Mal. That's why underneath the facade they resent us but could never show it. And they won't believe it when they read it if it's in print, etc. But they took a lot of shit from us because we were in such a shitty position. It was *hard* work and somebody had to take it. Those things are left out, about what bastards we were. Fuckin' big bastards, that's what the Beatles were. You have to be a bastard to make it, man. That's a fact, and the Beatles were the biggest bastards on earth. Like Allen's Christmas card says, "Yea, though I walk through the valley of the shadow of death, I will fear no evil, cause I'm the biggest bastard in the valley," or something. There's no kidding, if you make it, you're a bastard.

YOKO: But how did you manage to keep that clean image? It's amazing.

JOHN: Because everybody wants the image to carry on. The press around you want to carry on because they want the free drinks and the free whores and the fun. Everybody wants to keep on the bandwagon, it's *Satyricon*. We were the Caesar. Who was going to knock us when there's a million pounds to be made, all the handouts, the briberies, the police, all the fucking hype, you know? Everybody wanted in. That's why some of them are still trying to cling on to this. "Don't take it away from us. Don't take Rome from us. Not a portable Rome. We all have our houses and our cars and our lovers and our wives and office girls and parties and drink and drugs, don't take it from us." Otherwise, "You're mad, John, you're crazy, silly John wants to take all this away."

---

[49] *Love Me Do* was published by Penguin Books in 1964.

What do you say to Beatle people today?

You mean Beatle fans?

Yeah.

It depends who they are. If they ask me something about *Hard Day's* or *Help!*, I'm just straight with them and say, "Oh, it was good fun," or "It was like this." I'm giving you the dirt, but a lot of it was great fun. I don't know, I don't meet any Beatle people, do I [*laugh*]?

YOKO: No.

JOHN: I don't know where they are. In fact, I don't really know how to answer that. There's Apple scruffs, or whatever—I don't know what they are, Beatle people or not. I was referring back to what we were saying about the Beatles' influence around the time of *Revolver*. I'm saying like Dylan said it, "Don't follow leaders." He said it once.

What was it like in the early days in London?

When we came down, we were treated like provincials by the Cockneys.

What was it like, say, running around to discotheques with the Stones?

Oh, *that* was a great period. We were like King of the Jungle then. And we were very close to the Stones. I spent a lot of time with Brian [Jones] and Mick [Jagger], and I admired 'em, you know. I dug 'em the first time I saw 'em in whatever that place is they came from, Richmond Club. And spent a lot of time with 'em. It was great. We were *kings*, and we were all just at the prime, and we all used to just go around London in our cars and meet each other and talk about music with the Animals, Eric [Burdon], all that. It was really a good time. That was the best period fame wise. Where we were just—we didn't get mobbed so much, it was—I don't know, it was like—like a men's smoking club. Just a very good scene.

What was Brian like?

Brian Jones?

Yeah.

Well, he was different over the years as he disintegrated. He ended up the kind of guy that you dread he'd come on the phone, because you knew it was trouble. Or like that. He was really in a lot of pain. But in the early days he was alright, because he was young and good looking. But he's one of them guys that disintegrated in front of you. He wasn't sort of brilliant or anything, he was just a nice guy.

What did you feel when he died?[50]

By then I didn't feel anything, really. I just thought, "Another victim of the drugs." Like that.

What do you think of the Stones today?

I think it's a lot of hype. I like "Honky Tonk Women," and I think Mick's a *joke*, with all that fag dancing. I always did. I enjoy him, I mean I'm going to see his films and all that, like everybody else. But, *really*, I think it's a joke.

Do you see him much now?

No, I never do see him. We saw a bit of each other round when Allen was first coming in. I think Mick got *jealous*. I always was very respectful about Mick of the Stones, but he said a lot of sort of *tarty* things about the Beatles, which I am hurt by, because *I* can knock the

---

[50] Jones was found dead in his swimming pool on July 3, 1969; the coroner's report cited "death by misadventure."

Beatles, but don't let Mick Jagger knock them. Because I'd like to just *list* what we did and what the Stones did two months after, on every *fuckin'* album and every *fuckin'* thing we did, Mick does *exactly* the same. He imitates us. And I'd like *one* of you fuckin' underground people to point it out. *Let It Bleed.*[51]

YOKO: [*laugh*]

JOHN: *Satanic Majesties* is *Pepper*. "She's a Rainbow"[52]—it's the most fuckin' bullshit—that's "All You Need Is Love." I resent the implication that the Stones are like revolutionaries and that the Beatles weren't, you know? If the Stones were, or are, [then] the Beatles *really* were. They're not in the same class, music-wise or power-wise. Never were. And Mick always resented it. I never said anything, I always admired them because I like their funky music and I like their style. I always regretted cutting me hairs, a bit like that—

YOKO: You like rock & roll.

JOHN: Yeah, I like rock & roll, and I like the direction they took, after they got over trying to imitate us. But [Mick] is even going to do Apple now.[53] He's going to do the same thing. If it happens, he'll do exactly what we did and lose all his money. He's obviously *so* upset by how big the Beatles are compared to him, and he never got over it. He's now in his old age, and he's beginning to knock us. And he keeps knocking because now the Beatles are . . . like everybody jumped in on the bandwagon to knock Beatles when we split. And from Apple, the Apple facade, whatever was going on those days, that everybody's been

[51] The Stones' sardonic reply to *Let It Be*.

[52] The single from *Their Satanic Majesties Request*.

[53] At the time, the Stones were starting their own label, Rolling Stones Records.

knocking us. And I *resent* it, because even his first—second fuckin'
record, we *wrote* for him [*laugh*]. You know?

YOKO: And "Peace" made money and all that.[54]

JOHN: Which? Oh, he said "Peace" made money. We didn't make any
money from "Peace."

YOKO: No. We lost money.

*When 'Sgt. Pepper' came out did you know after you had put it together
that it was a great album? Did you feel that while you were making it?*

Yeah, yeah. And *Rubber Soul*, too. And *Revolver*. Yeah.

*What did you think of the review in the 'New York Times' of 'Sgt.
Pepper'?*

I don't remember it. Did it pan it?

Yeah.

I don't remember. Those days, reviews weren't that important
because we had it made, whatever happened. Nowadays, I'm sensitive
as shit, and every review counts. But those days, we were too big to
touch. I don't remember the reviews at all. I never read them, and we
were so blasé we never even read the news clippings. I didn't bother
with them or read anything about us. It was a *bore* to read about us.
Maybe Brian told us or somebody told us about it, that it was great or
lousy. I don't even remember ever hearing about it.

That was the first real anti-Beatles sentiment in the United States.

Yeah. Well, they have been trying to knock us down since we began,
including the British press, always saying . . . The big joke, in crowd
with us was, "What are you going to do when the bubble bursts?" And
we told them, privately, that we'd go when *we* decided, not when some

---

[54] The 1969 Plastic Ono Band single, "Give Peace a Chance."

fickle public decided. Because we're not a manufactured group. That we are what we are because we know what we're doing. Of course we made many mistakes and etc., etc. But we knew instinctively that it would end when we decided and not when the ATV decides to take off our series, or anything like that.[55] There were very few things that happened to Beatles that weren't really well thought out by us: whether to do it or not, what reaction, and would it last forever. We had an instinct for it, like somebody wrote.

We were talking about the tour 'Satyricon' and all, and then somehow the protection stopped. Like there's a story about George being at the party at which Mick and Keith were busted but they let George out.

I don't *believe* it, he wasn't there. I don't think he was there. Or it wasn't that they let him out, we were never protected like that. Only on the tours we were protected, because everybody was paid off. Then, I vaguely remember that George had left [the party]. There was a myth around that we were protected by the MBE. I don't know whether it was true, cause I still had it when they got me. Had I? When they busted me?[56]

YOKO: Um hum. Yes, you did.

---

[55] ATV was Lew Grade's entertainment company.

[56] In October 1968, John and Yoko were charged with possession of cannabis resin and obstructing police in the execution of a search warrant. The cannabis was discovered in a police raid on Ringo's London apartment, where John and Yoko were living temporarily. John later pled guilty to cannabis possession, but he and Yoko were found not guilty of obstruction.

JOHN: There's two ways of thinking, that they're out to get us, or it just happened that way. After I started *Two Virgins* and doing those kind of things, it was like, well, it seemed like I was fair game for the police.[57] There was some myth about us being protected because we had MBEs. I don't think it was true, it's just that we never did anything. I mean the way Paul said the acid thing—he never got attacked for it. I don't know if *that* was protected, because he was sort of openly admitting that we had drugs. I don't really know about that. I don't think we were ever protected in England. I just think nobody really bothered about us. I think George probably left that party hours before or the day before or something.

Whatever happened to Magic Alex?[58]

I don't know. He's still in London.

Did you all really think that he had these inventions?

I think some of his stuff actually has come true. I'll check it with Allen, but they just haven't manufactured a saleable object. He was just another guy that comes and goes round people like us. He's alright but he's cracked. He means well.

You say in the record that "freaks on the phone won't leave me alone."

Yeah.

"Don't gimme that brother, brother."

Right. Because I'm sick of all these aggressive hippies or whatever

---

[57] This 1968 album featured a controversial nude cover photo of John and Yoko.

[58] "Magic Alex" Mardas was a friend of the Beatles who worked for Apple, planning several far-fetched inventions, including an electronic device that would transmit the Maharishi's message around the world.

they are—the now generation—sort of being very uptight with me. Just either on the street or anywhere, on the phone or demanding my attention, as if I owe them something. I'm not their fucking parents. That's what it is. They come to the door with a fucking peace symbol and expect to just sort of march round the house or something, like an old Beatle fan. They're under a delusion of awareness by having long hair. And that's what I'm sick of. They frighten me. There's a lot of uptight maniacs going round wearing fuckin' peace symbols.

What did you think of [Charles] Manson when that thing happened?[59]

I don't know what I thought when it happened. I just think a lot of the things he says are true, that he's a child of the state made by us. And he took their children in when nobody else would, is what he did. But of course he's cracked, alright.

What were your feelings when he quoted "Helter Skelter"?

Well he's barmy. He's like any other Beatle kind of fan who reads mysticism into it. I mean we used to have a laugh—put in this, that or the other in a light-hearted way, that some intellectual would read as some symbolic youth generation whatsit. But we also took seriously some parts of the role. But I don't know what's "Helter Skelter" got to do with knifin' somebody, you know? I've never listened to the words properly, "helter skelter," which is sort of a noise.

Everybody was talking about the playing backwards thing on 'Abbey Road.'

---

[59] Charles Manson's "family" murdered seven people in August 1969. Manson had developed an apocalyptic theory that he claimed was based on the Beatles' 1968 "White Album." Manson claimed that the song "Helter Skelter" was a prophecy about an impending race war.

Well, that's bullshit. I've just read one about Dylan, too, that if you—
that he sings . . . I don't believe it, it's bullshit.

That rumor about Paul being dead . . .

I don't know where that started, that was barmy. I don't know, you
know as much about it as me.

Were any of those things on the album that they said were on the album?
Name a few.

A whole list of clues or . . .

No, that was bullshit, the whole thing was made up. We never went
for anything like that. We put *tit-tit-tit* in "Girl." It would be things like
a beat missing or something like that, see if anybody noticed—I know
we used to have a few things, but nothing that could be interpreted like
that.

Why do you think something like that whole death thing would happen?

Just people have got nothing better to do than study Bibles and
make nits about it and study rocks and make stories about how people
used to live and all that. It's just something to do for them. They live
vicariously.

*There's a point in which you decided that you'd give up your private life
and Yoko would give up her private life.*

No, we never decided to give up our private life, but we decided if
we're going to do anything like get married or like this film that we're
going to make now,[60] that we would dedicate it to peace, though on the

---

[60] At the time, John and Yoko were in New York making their avant-garde film
Up Your Legs Forever.

concept that peace—and during that period—because we are what we are. It evolved that somehow we ended up being responsible to produce peace. I mean even in our own heads we would get that way. But that's how it is. But peace is still important.

YOKO: Yes.

JOHN: But my life is dedicated to living, *surviving* is what it's about really, from day to day.

YOKO: We don't want to be hypocrites. Like most people start to destroy their own private life and just become like a big billboard saying "Peace," or something. But we want to try to be human as well, to try to hold on to our lives as well.

JOHN: We take on too much, that's the problem . . . I just won't get involved in too many things. I think [*laugh*]. I'll just do whatever happens. It's silly to feel guilty that I'm not working, I'm not doing this—it's just stupid. I'm just going to do what I want for meself. I mean for *both* of us.

What do you think the effects of events like the Bed-In were?

I don't know. I can't measure it.

YOKO: We don't know. You have to tell *us*.

JOHN: You tell us, *you're* reacting, we're acting. Somebody else has to tell us what the reaction is.

You recently visited Yoko's ex-husband, Tony Cox,[61] in Denmark, where you met a magician . . .

[61] Filmmaker Anthony Cox, Yoko's second husband, with whom she had a daughter, Kyoko, who lived with Cox.

Hamrick was brought over by Tony because he said this was a great doctor [who] was going to hypnotize us and we would stop smoking.[62]

YOKO: We thought that would be very practical.

JOHN: So we thought, great.

YOKO: Fantastic.

JOHN: So Tony said, "It really works cause it worked on us," and he said it was easy. So he was brought over and this guy comes in who seemed to be primaling all the time. He was always crying and that. And talking. And then we tried it, and it didn't work. We wanted a ciggie. He talked like crackers and then he said things like, well, he'd pull us back into our past lives. And we were game for anything then, you know? So I mean it's like going to a fortune teller. So we said, "Alright, do it." And he was mumbling, pretending to hypnotize us, and we're lying there, and he's making up all these Walt Disney stories about past lives, which we didn't believe. But he was such a nice guy in a way that we didn't want to say, "It seems a bit strange." And I was more into it than Yoko. She's not quite as silly as I am. But I was thinking, "Well, you never know, do you?" I had this thing, believe everything until it's disproved. And it turned from giving up ciggies into . . . and he was going on about he'd been on a spaceship. I said, "Well go on, tell us more."

YOKO: But you were a bit suspicious . . .

JOHN: I was suspicious, sure I was. But I wouldn't stop the stories

---

[62] Hamrick was a member of the "cosmic commune," the Harbingers (and a friend of Anthony Cox), who tried to hypnotize John and Yoko so that they could quit smoking cigarettes.

coming out, "Tell us how it was." And then he'd be saying how they all think they're . . . There was this Harbinger . . . But they were obviously all insane people. And then these other two came with him—I don't know what they wanted—one in purple and the other a magician. He said he was going to put spells on everybody and all that—just really crazy. And we were getting worried by then, it was gettin' out of hand. All of them think they're higher beings, I mean they're still traveling around Europe and everywhere thinking they've got messages. It's a shame [laugh]. And Hamrick said he'd been on a flying saucer, but we always suspected with somebody so spiritual or whatever the shit, why is he so fat, why can't he get that together? That was the thing. And he'd say, "Well, because I have to get myself in a certain state of being by eating all these ice cream buns to communicate with the Martians." The poor old dear and his wife are probably up in Canada now. So actually we went [to Denmark] to talk to—to see Kyoko.

You once said that talking is a bad form of communication. Music is a better form.

When did I say that? I don't know if it's true or not. It's true one minute and not true the next.

What do you think the future of rock & roll is?

Whatever we make it. I mean, if we want to go bullshitting off into intellectualism with rock & roll, we're going to get bullshitting rock intellectualism. If we want *real* rock & roll, it's up to all of us to create it. And stop being hyped by revolutionary image and long hair. We've got to get over *that* bit. That's what cutting hair's about. Let's own up now and see who's who and who's doing something about what. And who's making music and who's laying down bullshit. Rock & roll will be whatever we make it.

Why do you think it means so much to people?

Rock & roll? Because it's primitive enough and it has no bullshit—the best stuff. And it gets *through* to you. It's beat. Go to the jungle and they have the rhythm, throughout the world. It's as simple as that. You get the rhythm going, everybody gets into it. I read that Malcolm X or Eldridge Cleaver or somebody said that, with rock, the blacks gave the middle-class whites back their bodies, put their minds and bodies to it. It's something like that. It gets through. To me it got through. It was the only thing that could get through to me out of all the things that were happening when I was fifteen. Rock & roll was real. Everything else was unreal. And the thing about rock & roll, good rock & roll, whatever good means, etc., ha-ha, and all *that* shit, is that it's *real*. And realism gets through to you, *despite* yourself. You recognize something in it which is true, like all true art. *Whatever art is*, readers. Okay? It's that. If it's real, it's simple usually. And if it's simple, it's true. Something like that.

YOKO: Um.

JOHN: Rock & roll got through to you [Yoko], didn't it?

YOKO: Yes . . .

JOHN: Finally.

YOKO: Classical music was basically 4/4, and then it went into 4/3, too, which is a waltz, rhythm and all that. But it just went further and further away from the heartbeat. Heartbeat is 4/4, and it goes—[*demonstrates*] you know? And then they started 1–2–3, all that. And then . . .

JOHN: Perversion.

YOKO: . . . rhythm became very decorative and then you know like

Schoenberg, Webern, all their rhythm is like—[*demonstrates*] you know like that. It's highly complicated and interesting, and our minds are very much like that, but they lost the heartbeat. I went to see the Beatles' session in the beginning and I thought, "Oh, well." So I was saying to John, "Well, why do you always use that beat all the time? The same beat. Why don't you do something a bit more complex?"

JOHN: I was doing "Bulldog."

YOKO: And he was saying, "Oh, she's saying we're using the same beat all the time."

JOHN: Very embarrassing.

YOKO: And then I suddenly realized, that's what . . .

Embarrassing for yourself or for Yoko?

JOHN: For me, cause if somebody starts playing that intellectual on me, I'm going to say, "Oh, maybe . . ."

YOKO: He's a very shy fellow . . .

JOHN: I'm shy. If somebody attacks, I shrink.

YOKO: Um.

JOHN: Until I've got . . .

YOKO: I had the same intellectual snobbery . . .

JOHN: She's an intellectual, supreme intellectual. You see, I really know what I'm talking about when I say, "those fuckin' intellectuals." They have to have a sort of maths-formula thought pattern, in their head to feel something. They have to go, "This is the result of that, which did this," because the programming of when they were children.

YOKO: The best way to explain it, I can't play the piano unless I see a score.

JOHN: Which is *insanity*.

YOKO: I have to first see—so that's that.

JOHN: *That* is intellectualism.

YOKO: [*laugh*]

JOHN: And that is musicianship, that's the school of music shit—to not be able to make music unless you can read a piece of paper, which has nothing to do with music.

And you feel the same way about rock & roll now at thirty as you did at fifteen?

Well, it'll never be as new. It's never going to do what it did to me then. But "Tutti Frutti" or "Long Tall Sally"[63] is pretty avant garde. I met an old avant-garde friend of Yoko's in the Village the other day who was talking about "one note," and "didn't Dylan sing one note?"—like he's just discovered that. That's about as far out as you can get. Intellectually I can play games enough to [devise] reasons why that music is very important and always will be. Like the blues as opposed to jazz—white middle-class good jazz as opposed to the blues. The blues is better.

Because it's simpler?

Cause it's *real*. It's not perverted or thought—it's not a concept. It is a chair, not a design for a chair or a better chair or a bigger chair or a chair with leather or with design. It is the first chair, it's chairs for sitting on, not chairs for looking at or being appreciated. You *sit* on that music.

How would you describe Beatles music?

Well, it means a lot of things to me. There's not *one* thing that's Beatle music, because I'm part of it. What is Beatle music, "Walrus" or "Penny Lane?" Which? It's that diverse. Or "I Want to Hold Your Hand" or "Revolution 9"?

What do you think it was about "Love Me Do" . . .

---

63 Little Richard's Number Six hit single from 1956.

"Love Me Do" was rock & roll. Pretty funky.

What do you think accounted for the sudden popularity of "Love Me Do"?

"Love Me Do" was never big. It might have made it over here, after we'd made it. Remember that America followed much after. Because we were local heroes. "Love Me Do" didn't only make Number Forty on the charts in England, it didn't do anything.

What was it about the sound, not just "Love Me Do" but anything from that period, that caught everybody?

Because we didn't sound like everybody else, that's all. We didn't sound like the black musicians because we weren't black and because we were brought up on a different kind of music and atmosphere. And so "Please Please Me" and "From Me to You" and all those were our version of the chair. We were building our own chairs, that's all, and they were sort of local chairs. I don't know.

What were the first devices and tricks that you used to embellish . . .

The first gimmick was the harmonica. There'd been a few songs "Hey! Baby," and there was a terrible thing called "I Remember You" in England.[64] And I played a lot of harmonica, mouth organ really, when I was a child. So we did those numbers. So we started using it on "Love Me Do," just for arrangement, because we used to work out arrangements. We just used it. And then we stuck it on "Please Please Me" and then we stuck it on "From Me to You," like that. It went on and on, it got into the gimmick, and then we dropped it. It got embarrassing.

---

[64] "Hey! Baby" was a Number One hit for Bruce Channel in 1962; "I Remember You" was a Number Five hit for Frank Ifield in 1962 and had been a Number Nine hit for Jimmy Dorsey in 1942.

What sort of complexities or embellishment besides harmonica did you start to use?

Well . . . we did that at the Cavern. I was playing harmonica, and that was the gimmick in the early days was the harmonica. I don't know what you mean—musically on the records?

On records.

The first sort of tricks was double tracking on the second album, we discovered that, or it was told to us, "You can do this." That really set the ball rolling. We double tracked ourselves off the album on the second album.[65] Apart from that, the first lot, we just did as a group that went in and played and they put it on tape and we left. They remixed it, they did everything to it. I would love to remix some of the early stuff, because it's *better* than it sounds.

YOKO: And I want to cover some of John's songs.

JOHN: Yes, yes, yes. She's going to do a Lennon–McCartney album. But you've got to do your old . . . she's got so many albums to do.

Have you ever thought if there's a live album?

Yeah, Hollywood Bowl—it was pretty tatty. It's nice to hear. It'll probably go out one day, I suppose. But we were *so* nervous. Dean Martin was in the audience and all their children. It wasn't like people anymore. It was like that. And we were always nervous—it was like going on the Palladium.[66] But we were there alright. There's also Shea Stadium somewhere. There's one in Italy apparently that somebody

---

[65] 1963's *With the Beatles*.

[66] On October 16, 1963, the Beatles appeared on television for the first time on Britain's then top-rated program, *Val Parnell's Sunday Night at the London Palladium*.

recorded there. But you always did everything twenty times faster than normal.

What do you think of those concerts, like the Hollywood Bowl?

It was awful. Hated it. Some of them were good, some weren't. I didn't like Hollywood Bowl. If we knew we were being recorded, it was *death*, we were so frightened. And because you knew it was always terrible: You could never hear yourself and you knew that they were fucking it up on the tape anyway. There was no bass, and they never recorded the drums, you can never hear them. The places were built for fuckin' orchestras, not groups. Some of those big gigs were good but not many of them.

In re-reading an interview you did with Jon Cott, you said something about "Ticket to Ride" being a favorite song of yours.

Yeah, I liked it, cause it was slightly a new sound at the time.

In what way?

Because it was pretty fuckin' heavy for then. If you go and look in the charts for what other music people were making, and you hear it now, it doesn't sound too bad. It's one of them. It doesn't make you cringe.

YOKO: It's very heavy.

JOHN: If you'd give me the eight-track now, remix it—I'll show you what it is *really*, but you can hear it there. I used to like guitars. I don't want anything else on the album, the guitars and janglin' piano or whatever. It's all happening, it's a heavy record. And the drums are heavy too. That's why I like it.

What part did you ever play in the songs that are heavily identified with Paul, like "Yesterday"?

"Yesterday" I had nothing to do with.

"Eleanor Rigby"?

"Eleanor Rigby" I wrote a good half of the lyrics or more.

When did Paul show you "Yesterday"?

I don't remember—I really don't remember, it was a long time ago. I think he was . . . I really don't remember, it just sort of appeared.

Who do you think has done the best versions of your stuff?

I can't think of anybody.

Did you hear Ike and Tina Turner doing "Come Together"?

Yeah, I think they did too much of a job on it. I think they could have done it better. They did a better "Honky Tonk Women."

Ray Charles doing "Yesterday"?

That was quite nice.

And you had Otis doing "Day Tripper," what did you think of that?

I don't think he did a very good job on "Day Tripper." I never went much for the covers. It doesn't interest me, really. I like people doing them—I've heard some nice versions of "In My Life," I don't know who it was, though [Judy Collins]. José Feliciano did "Help!" quite nice once. I like people doing it, I get a kick out of it. I think it was interesting that Nina Simone did a sort of answer to "Revolution." That was very good—it was sort of like "Revolution," but not quite. That I sort of enjoyed, somebody who reacted immediately to what I had said.

Who wrote "Nowhere Man"?

Me, me.

Did you write that about anybody in particular?

Probably about myself. I remember I was just going through this paranoia trying to write something and nothing would come out, so I just lay down and tried to not write and then this came out, the whole thing came out in one gulp.

What songs really stick in your mind as being Lennon–McCartney songs?

"I Want to Hold Your Hand," "From Me to You," "She Loves You"—I'd have to have the list, there's so many, trillions of 'em. Those are the ones. In a rock band you have to make singles, you have to keep writing them. Plenty more. We both had our fingers in each other's pies.

I remember that the simplicity on the new album was evident on the Beatles' double album. It was evident on "She's So Heavy," in fact a reviewer wrote of "She's So Heavy": "He seems to have lost his talent for lyrics, it's so simple and boring." "She's So Heavy" was about Yoko. When it gets down to it, like she said, when you're drowning you don't say, "I would be incredibly pleased if someone would have the foresight to notice me drowning and come and help me," you just *scream*. And in "She's So Heavy" I just sang, "I want you, I want you so bad, she's so heavy, I want you," like that. I started simplifying my lyrics then, on the double album.

A song from the 'Help!' album, like "You've Got to Hide Your Love Away," how did you write that? What were the circumstances? Where were you?

I was in Kenwood and I would just be songwriting. The period would be for songwriting and so every day I would attempt to write a song, and it's one of those that you sort of sing a bit sadly to yourself, "Here I stand, head in hand . . . "

I started thinking about my own emotions—I don't know when exactly it started, like "I'm a Loser" or "Hide Your Love Away" or those kind of things—instead of projecting myself into a situation, I would try to express what I felt about myself which I'd done in me books. I think it was Dylan helped me realize that—not by any discussion or anything but just by hearing his work—I had a sort of professional songwriter's attitude to writing pop songs; he would turn out a certain style of song for a single and we would do a certain style of thing for this and the other thing. I was already a stylized songwriter on the first album. But to express myself I would write *Spaniard in the Works* or *In His Own Write*, the personal stories which were expressive of my personal emotions.[67] I'd have a separate songwriting John Lennon who wrote songs for the sort of meat market, and I didn't consider them—the lyrics or anything—to have any depth at all. They were just a joke. Then I started being me about the songs, not writing them objectively, but subjectively.

What about on 'Rubber Soul'—"Norwegian Wood"?

I was trying to write about an affair without letting me wife know I was writing about an affair, so it was very gobbledegook. I was sort of writing from my experiences, girls' flats, things like that.

Where did you write that?

I wrote it at Kenwood.

When did you decide to put a sitar on it?

I think it was at the studio. George had just got the sitar and I said, "Could you play this piece?" We went through many different sort of versions of the song, it was never right and I was getting very angry about it, it wasn't coming out like I said. They said, "Just do it how you want to do it," and I said, "I just want to do it like this." They let me go and I did the guitar very loudly into the mike and sang it at the

---

[67] Lennon's books *In His Own Write* (1964) and *A Spaniard in the Works* (1965) included prose, poetry and drawings.

same time, and then George had the sitar and I asked him could he play the piece that I'd written, *dee diddley dee diddley dee*, that bit—and he was not sure whether he could play it yet because he hadn't done much on the sitar but he was willing to have a go, as is his wont, and he learned the bit and dubbed it on after. I think we did it in sections.

You also have a song on that album, "In My Life." When did you write that?

I wrote that in Kenwood. I used to write upstairs where I had about ten Brunell tape recorders all linked up—I still have them. I'd mastered them over the period of a year or two. I could never make a rock & roll record, but I could make some far-out stuff on it. I wrote it upstairs, that was one where I wrote the lyrics first and then sang it. That was usually the case with things like "In My Life" and "Universe" and some of the ones that stand out a bit.

Would you just record yourself and a guitar on a tape and then bring it in to the studio?

I would do that just to get an impression of what it sounded like *sung* and to hear it back for judging it—you never know til you hear the song yourself. I would double track the guitar or the voice or something on the tape. I think on "Norwegian Wood" and "In My Life" Paul helped with the middle eight, to give credit where it's due.

From the same period, same time, I never liked "Run for Your Life," because it was a song I just knocked off. It was inspired—this is a very vague connection—from "Baby Let's Play House." There was a line on it—I used to like specific lines from songs—"I'd rather see you dead, little girl, then to be with another man"—so I wrote it around that, but I didn't think it was that important. "Girl" I liked because I was, in a way, trying to say something or other about Christianity, which I was opposed to at the time.

Why Christianity in that song?

Because I was brought up in the church. One of the reviews of *In His Own Write* was that they tried to put me in this satire boom with Peter Cook and those people that came out to Cambridge, saying, "He's just satirizing the normal things like the church and the state," which is what I did in *In His Own Write*.[68] Those are the things that you keep satirizing because they're the only things. I was pretty heavy on the church in both books, but it was never picked up, although it was obviously there. I was just talking about Christianity in that . . . a thing like you have to be tortured to attain heaven. I'm only saying that I was talking about "pain will lead to pleasure" in "Girl" and that was the Catholic Christian concept—to be tortured and then it'll be alright, which seems to be a bit true but not in their concept of it. But I didn't believe in that, that you *have* to be tortured to attain anything, it just so happens that you were.

Let me ask you about one on the double album, "Glass Onion." You set out to write a little message to the audience.

Yeah, I was having a laugh because there'd been so much gobbledegook about *Pepper*, play it backwards and you stand on your head and all that. Even now, I just saw Mel Torme on TV the other day saying that "Lucy" was written to promote drugs and so was "A Little Help From My Friends" and none of them were at all. "A Little Help From My Friends" only says get high in it. It's really about a little help from my

---

[68] Actor/comedian Peter Cook was one of the original members of the comedy troupe that created the groundbreaking satiric revue "Beyond the Fringe."

friends, it's a sincere message. Paul had the line about "little help from my friends." I'm not sure, he had some kind of structure for it and—we wrote it pretty well fifty-fifty but it was based on his original idea.

In "I Am the Walrus" . . .

That was the B side of "Hello, Goodbye," can you believe it?

You say in "Glass Onion": "here's another clue for you all . . . "

"The Walrus is Paul."

Paul.

Ray Coleman asked me.[69] At that time, [I was] still in my love cloud with Yoko, I felt, well, you know, I'll just say something nice to Paul, that it's alright and, "You did a good job over these few years holding us together." He was trying to organize the group and that, and do the music and be an individual artist and all that stuff. I wanted to say something to him. And I did it for that reason. I thought, "Well, you can *have* it, I've got Yoko, and thank you, you can have the credit."

And now you've decided . . .

I decided I'm sick of reading things about Paul is the musician and George is the philosopher and I wonder where I fit in. What was my contribution? I get hurt. I'm sick of it. I'd sooner be like [Frank] Zappa and say, "Listen, you fuckers, this is what I did. And I don't care whether you like my attitude saying it, but that's what I am, I'm a fuckin' artist, man." And I'm *not* a fuckin' PR agent or the product of some other person's imagination, whether you're the public or whatever. I'm standing by my work, whereas before I would not stand by it. So that's what I'm saying. *I* was the walrus, whatever that means. We

---

[69] A *Melody Maker* writer who traveled with the Beatles and interviewed John many times. He later wrote the 1984 book *Lennon: The Definitive Biography*.

saw the movie in L.A. and the walrus was a big capitalist that ate all the fuckin' oysters [*laugh*], if you must know. That's what he was. I always had this image of "The Walrus and the Carpenter"[70]—and I never checked what the walrus was. I've been going around and saying, "I'm the walrus," that it's something, but he's a fucking bastard [*laugh*]. That's what it turns out to be. The way it's written everybody presumes that it *means* something. I mean even I did, so I mean we all just presumed, just cause I said, "I am the walrus" that it must mean I am *God* or something, but it's just poetry. But it became symbolic with me.

What other little things are there like that?

The walrus—oh, I don't know. I said hello to Peter Brown in "The Ballad of John and Yoko." It's just a way of thanking them. Because I learned things from Yoko in a way. They always dedicate their work, these avant-garde people, to each other, like this is for [the pianist] David Tudor and this is for that. And they're great for the original, the whole book's dedicated to all these men, and I wouldn't let her put it in the real one. But now I understand it a bit. I thought they were all sort of . . .

YOKO: No, it wasn't anything special . . .

JOHN: No, I know. Like I dedicated the album to Yoko, but they dedicated it like, "Isolation" for George, or "Isolation" for Jann . . . Just because you were around when we spoke, or something like that. It's *nice* that they did that to each other, and so it's a bit like that.

YOKO: With a drop of a hat they did . . .

---

[70] John and Yoko saw the film version of *Alice in Wonderland*; Lewis Carroll also wrote "The Walrus and the Carpenter."

JOHN: Yes, yes, yes. Yes. I understand, he understands, don't worry. They were just in a group and they did a lot of that, so I just sort of picked up on it, I suppose. I want people to love me. I want to be loved.

What did you think of 'Abbey Road'?

I liked the A side. I never liked that sort of pop opera on the other side, I think it's *junk*.

It seemed very fragmented . . .

Yeah, because it was just bits of song thrown together. And I can't remember what some of it is. "Come Together" is alright. And some things on it.

"Come Together"—was that you?

Yeah, that was *my* song. That's all I remember. Did I do anything else on *Abbey Road*? [*singing "Come Together"*] It couldn't be an album with just one track on it.

YOKO: No, no, no.

JOHN: Anyway I . . . it was a competent album, like *Rubber Soul* in a way, it was together in that way, but it had no life really.

How did you come to write "Come Together"?

I can't say this, we're being sued, you see. See, the Learys wanted me to write—this is not the suing bit—them a campaign song.[71] And their slogan was "come together." I wrote it, I've still got it, it's actually very like the Kinks—[*sings*] "Dra-a-a-a-g," you know, some song of theirs. But anyway, I wrote "Come Together." But before I wrote their song, I was writing in the office, just sort of . . . I can't say this because we're going to get sued because it's silly. I was writing this like, "You Can't Catch Me,"

---

[71] Dr. Timothy and his fourth wife Rosemary;. Leary was a candidate for governor of California in 1970.

the same rhythm and I'm using the old words.[72] I often do it, if I'm trying to write one like "Long Tall Sally" or I'm just singing, I'm going, [sings] "oh, gonna tell Mary," and just make up—parodize the words, I was doing that. And then when I got . . . I stopped and I said—just came out—"come together," cause "come together" was rolling around in me head. "Right now, over me." Now "over me" was meant to be like a joke—but "oh—oh-ver me," like Elvis used to "o-o-o-ver you." And then I never put the other [one out]—the other one went, [sings] "come together, and [claps in rhythm] join the party, co-o-ome together and join the party." For Leary—like "Give Peace a Chance," a chant along thing.

YOKO: Leary doesn't know, but I wish you'd send that to him.

JOHN: Yeah, I know, but I never get around to it. So I never did it, and I ended up writing "Come Together" instead. And they're suing me because it's like "You Can't Catch Me," for the first half a line or something, because Chuck Berry's words went something like that. But anyway, it's not *him* that's suing me, it's his people. So you have to not put that in because they'll say, "Oh there, he admitted it." And I think it's a *compliment* to Chuck Berry, not a fucking . . . [laugh]—I mean we resurrected him.

---

72   The owner of the song's copyright, Big Seven Music Corporation, owned by the notorious Morris Levy, filed suit against Lennon for copyright infringement in 1969, claiming that he used a few of the 1956 Chuck Berry song's lines in "Come Together." The suit finally settled in 1973 in the publisher's favor, and to compensate Levy, Lennon agreed to record three songs owned by his publishing company. (Lennon was recording *Rock 'n' Roll*, a collection of his favorite songs of the Fifties and Sixties.) Levy actually released a bootleg version of *Rock 'n' Roll* prior to its official 1975 release; Lennon sued Levy this time and won.

Like in "All You Need Is Love" . . .

Many songs are similar, [and] I always like to say where the source was. I say, "Well, that was 'You Can't Catch Me.'" But if I never said it, nobody'd ever know. Just one guy spotted it.

What was it like recording "Instant Karma"? That was your first record with Phil [Spector].

It was great, cause I wrote it in the morning on the piano, like I said many times, and I went to the office and I sang it. I thought, "Hell, let's do it," and we booked the studio. And Phil came in, he said, "How do you want it?" I said, "You know, 1950 but now." And he said "Right," and *boom*, I did it in just about three goes. He played it back, and there it was. I said, "A bit more bass," that's all. And off we went. See, Phil doesn't fuss about with fuckin' stereo or all the bullshit. Just "Did it sound alright? Let's have it." It doesn't matter whether something's prominent or not prominent. If it sounds good to you as a layman or as a human, *take* it. Don't bother whether this is like that or the quality of this. That suits me fine. [*To someone entering the room*] Yeah, we're just finishing. Have we finished?

I'd like to know more, but we can take a break. I'd like to call Annie and have her come over.[73]

Oh, I don't want to, I don't want to, *really*. Cause nobody's done it, I don't want to start all that pictures of John and Yoko bit. Just take one with an Instamatic, you can take it.

---

[73] Photographer Annie Leibovitz had just that year started working for ROLLING STONE; she eventually photographed Lennon (and Yoko Ono) for the covers of the issues that ran this interview in two parts, on January 21, 1971, and February 4, 1971.

It'll be terrible. I just want to take a—

It won't be terrible.

I want to get a good picture for the cover.

Look at the album. Well, look—take it. Don't be a snob, don't be professional. Just take a photo.

[*break*]

When did you first become aware of the idea of stereo? Of being able to work in stereo?

Oh, some time or other, I don't know. There was a period where we started realizing that you can go and remix it yourself. And we started listening to them or saying, "Well, why couldn't you do that?" We'd just standing by the [control] board saying, "Oh, well, what about that?" And George [Martin] would say, "Well, how do you like this?" From the early days, they just would present us with finished product. We'd say, "What happened to the bass?" or something. They'd say, "Oh well, that's how it is." That kind of thing. It must have been a gradual thing.

Was 'Rubber Soul' the first album where you took control?

I think so, full control. Well, we'd take control, we'd say, "This is what I want on mine. And it should be like that, etc. etc." I'm guessing. If it sounds like it, that's when it happened. There's an obvious difference in the . . .

What did you think of "Give Peace a Chance"?

As a record?

Yeah.

I thought it was beautiful.

Did you see the Moratorium Day in Washington?[74]

Oh yeah, that's what it was for. I think I heard . . . I don't know, I just remember hearing them all singing. I don't know whether it was on the radio or TV, but that was a very big moment for me. That's what the song was about, because I'm shy *and* aggressive. So I have great hopes for what I do, my work. And I also have great despair that it's all pointless and shit—how can you top Beethoven or Shakespeare or whatever. And in me secret heart I wanted to write something that would take over "We Shall Overcome." I don't know why, that's the one they always sang. I thought, "Why isn't somebody writing one for the people *now*?" That's what my job is. Our job is to write for the people *now*. So the songs that they go and sing on their buses are not just love songs. I have the same kind of hope for "Working Class Hero," but I know it's a different concept. I think it's a revolutionary song—it's really just revolutionary. I just think its concept is revolutionary. I hope it's for workers and *not* for tarts and fags. I hope it's about what "Give Peace a Chance" was about. But I don't know—on the other hand, it might just be ignored. I think it's for the people like me who are working class, who are supposed to be processed into the middle classes, or into the machinery. It's *my* experience, and I hope it's just a warning to people, "Working Class Hero."

YOKO: That's a fantastic song!

JOHN: No, I don't want praise, I just—I'm saying I think it's a revolutionary song. Not the song itself, it's a song for the revolution.

---

[74] In 1969, the New Mobilization Committee to End the War organized a three-day nationwide antiwar demonstration, culminating in a massive march in Washington, D.C., on November 15.

Can you deliberately put out a commercial record—do you have a feeling for a Number One record?

No. See, I keep thinking "Mother" is a commercial record, because all the time I was writing it, it was the one I was singing the most and it's the one that seemed to catch on in my head. I'm convinced that "Mother" is a commercial record. But—

I agree.

You agree? Well, thank you. But you said *"God"* . . .

No, I didn't.

No, no, well they're all playing "God." Or "Isolation."

You're right about "Mother" because it's the one that I have in my head all the time.

Yeah, right.

Trust your instinct. Put that out.

Yeah, but it's the politics in it, too. Politics will prepare the ground for my album. The same as "My Sweet Lord" prepared the ground for George's [*All Things Must Pass*]. I'm not going to get hits just like that. People aren't going to buy my album just cause ROLLING STONE liked it. People have got to be *hyped* in a way, they've got to have it presented to them in all the best ways possible. And if "Love" can—because I like the song "Love." I like the melody and the words and everything, I think it's beautiful. I'm more of a rocker, that's all. I originally conceived of "Mother" and "Love" as being a single, but I want to put one out with her [Yoko]. Then I have to get rid of one. But I think "Love" will do me more good.

I don't think so. I say, trust your instinct . . . "Mother"—that's what it is. What will stay in your head the longest?

No, but if you hear "Love" more, that will stay in your head more. "Love" is also commercial.

I've heard it all the same number of times, and "Mother" is the one I always have in mind.

Yeah, I understand that. If you just take "Love," it's a single song, it's a single record. "Mother" is a single, "Love" is a single. "God" could be. So could "Isolation," and "Remember."

YOKO: And "Working Class Hero."

JOHN: I write singles, I write them all the same way. But [with] "Mother"—you've got to take into account the lyrics, too. If I can capture more sales by singing about love than singing about my mother, I'll do it.

YOKO: Because that would open a door for . . .

I understand—

JOHN: I'm opening a door for John Lennon, not for music or for the Beatles or for a movement or anything. I'm presenting myself to as broad a scope as I can. And I'm talking out what I think, as a result of them saying this to me. There's also many little sidelines—this is not for publication—like Capitol was trying to say that this isn't a Plastic Ono record. But that has nothing to do with "Love" actually. [The label is] trying to now say that this is John Lennon, one of the Beatles. And therefore it's a different deal, you see. When they were on the McCartney bandwagon, which they were on, and they thought that I was just an idiot pissing about with a Japanese broad and the music we were making, like *Toronto*, they didn't want to put out, because they didn't like that.[75] They were content to let me be a Plastic Ono Band and give me a release on it, a special release I have

[75] *Live Peace in Toronto, 1969*, recorded live at a rock festival, included experimental tracks by Yoko.

to get. Because Beatles are tied up as *Beatles* or as individual performers.

What are the implications?

The implications are that money—all of it's money, man. They're saying well, "Looks like this is a John Lennon album, not Plastic Ono." Well, to me, it's Plastic Ono, or I wouldn't put it out like that [on flipsides of a single]. So that's another reason to put us out together like that. There's all those things. But I'm going to think about "Love." You see, the original idea was there's not enough things on the album to put out a single. Because there's only ten[76] songs or nine if you don't count "Mummy."[77] And that means that there's nothing to buy then. But to me it sounds like there's forty songs on it.

YOKO: Very heavy.

JOHN: But there's that side of the market. I'm not going to *disregard* it. I mean to sell as *many* albums as I can, as *many* records as I possibly can because I'm an artist who wants everybody to love me and *everybody* to buy my stuff. And I'll go for *that*. Without selling out anymore.

The theory of putting out something that's commercial to get people to buy the album of course is obvious. There's no great shakes about that theory but the question is which is most commercial, "Love" or "Mother"?

How quick do you get to Number One? The thing is, "Love" will attract more people because of the message, man. Many, many people will not like "Mother"; it hurts them. The first thing that happens to you when you get the album is you can't take it. Everybody's reacted exactly the same. They think, "*fuck!*" That's how everybody is. And the second time,

---

[76]   Actually there are eleven tracks on *Plastic Ono Band*.

[77]   "My Mummy's Dead," the last song on *Plastic Ono Band*.

they start saying, "Oh, well, there's a little . . ." so I can't lay "Mother" on them. It confirms the suspicions that something nasty's going on with that John Lennon and his broad again. People aren't that hip. Students aren't that aware and all that bullshit. They're just like anybody else. "Oh, oh misery, is that what it's . . . don't tell me I'm . . . it is really awful."

YOKO: "Why is he accusing his mother?"

JOHN: "Be a good boy now, John." Or "you had a hard time but *me*, me and my mother . . ." So there's all that to go through. "Love" I wrote in a spirit of love. In all that shit, I wrote it in a spirit of love. It's for Yoko, it has all that connotation for me. It's a beautiful melody and I'm not even *known* for writing melody. There's that angle. Also, people would hear it and they've heard all this shit about "it's banned and he doesn't believe in God or the Kennedys and—my God, what's he"—all that. I'm going to get that, you know. This will say, "Well, in amongst that in life, there is that, but there's that too." I'm very good [laughing], I've really convinced meself there.

YOKO: But it's true—that's a very good thing.

JOHN: I mean, *whoo*, yes. But I'll still consider it.

YOKO: People think "Mother" is too personal.

JOHN: It'll do me good. If it goes, it'll do me good. Go on.[78]

Did you write most of the songs on this album on guitar or piano?

The ones where I play guitar I wrote on guitar. The ones where I play piano I wrote on piano.

What do you think is the difference between a piano song and a guitar song?

[78] "Mother" actually became the album's single, released January 9, 1971; it wasn't a hit, peaking at Number 43.

Well, let's think of the difference between "I Found Out" and "Remember." There's more piano ones on this one than [on] guitar.

What are the differences to you when you write them?

Because I play piano even worse than I play guitar, that's a limited palette, as they call it. So I surprise meself. I have to think in terms of, go from C to A, and I'm not quite sure where I am half the time. When I'm holding the chord, I go *ding* and it might only be an ordinary—on the guitar it's only a sixth or a seventh [chord]. On the piano, I don't know what it is. So it's that kind of feel about it. But I know such a lot about the guitar. With guitar I can be buskin'. If I want to write just a rocker, I have to play guitar cause I can't play piano well enough to inspire me to rock. It's like that. That's the difference really.

What do you think are your best songs?

Ever? Ever?

Ever. What is the best song?

The *one* best song?

Have you thought of that?

I don't know, you see, somebody asked me what's my favorite song, is it "Stardust" or something like that. I can't—that kind of decision making I can't make. I like—I always like "Walrus," "Strawberry Fields," "Help!," "In My Life." Those are some favorites.

Why "Help!"?

Because I *mean* it. It's real. The lyric is as good now as it was then. It's not different. It makes me feel secure to know that I was that sensible or whatever—not sensible but aware of myself then. That's with no acid, no nothing, well, pot, or whatever. It was just me singing "Help!" and I meant it. I don't like the *recording* that much. The *song* I like. We did it too fast to try and be commercial and all that. I like "I Want to

Hold Your Hand." We wrote that together—it's a beautiful melody. I might do "I Want to Hold Your Hand" and "Help!" again, because I like them. I sing them, they're the kind of songs I sing [*laugh*].

Why "Strawberry Fields"? Again, cause that was real?

Because it's real, yeah. It was real for then, and it's like talking. "I sometimes think no but I—then again I mean I sa—you know," like that.[79] It's like that Elton John one where he talks to himself, sort of singing, which I thought was nice. It reminded me of that.

Songs like "Girl"?

Yeah, I like that one.

"Run for Your Life"?

"Run for Your Life" I always hated.

Why?

I don't know. Because it was one of those I knocked off just to write a song. It was phony, but "Girl" is real. There's no such thing as the girl, she was a dream. But the words are alright. It's about, well, "she taught when she was young that pain would lead to pleasure, did she understand it," all that. They're sort of philosophy quotes. It was reasonable. I was thinking about it when I wrote it. It wasn't just *a* song. It was about that girl that happened to turn out to be Yoko in the end, but the one that a lot of us were looking for. There are many songs I forget like that, that I *do* like. I like "Across the Universe," too.

Why?

It's one of the best lyrics I've written. In fact, it could be *the* best. It's one of the best. It's good poetry, or whatever you call it. Without tune,

[79] Actual lyric is: "Always, no sometimes, think it's me, but you know I know when it's a dream."

it stands. The ones I like are ones that stand as words, without melody. They don't have to have any melody. It's a poem, you could read them.

That's your ultimate criterion?

No, it's just the ones I happen to like. I like to read other people's lyrics, too.

So what happened with 'Let It Be'?

Well, it was another one like *Magical Mystery Tour* that . . . [*sigh*] well, sort of—this is—it's hard to say. In a nutshell, Paul wanted to make—it was time for another Beatle movie or something, and Paul wanted us to go on the road or do something. As usual, George and I were going, "Oh, we don't want to do it, fuck," and all that. He set it up and there was all discussions about where to go and all that. I would just tag along and I had Yoko by then, I didn't even give a shit about anything. I was stoned all the time, too, on H, etc. And I just didn't give a shit. And nobody did, you know. Anyway, it's like in the movie when I go to do "Across the Universe," Paul yawns and plays boogie, and I merely say, "Oh, anybody want to do a fast one?" That's how I am. Year after year, that begins to wear you down.

How long did those sessions last?

Oh, fuckin'—God knows how long. Paul had this idea that we were going to rehearse or . . . see it all was more like Simon and Garfunkel [*laugh*], like looking for perfection all the time. And so he has these ideas that we'll rehearse and then make the album. And of course we're lazy fuckers and we've been playing for twenty years, for fuck's sake, we're grown men, we're not going to sit around rehearsing. I'm not, anyway. And we couldn't get into it. And we put down a few tracks and nobody was in it at all. It was a dreadful, dreadful feeling in Twickenham Studio, and being filmed all the time. I just wanted them to go away, and we'd be there, eight in the morning. You couldn't make music at eight in the morning or ten or whatever it was, in a strange place with people filming you and colored lights.

How did it end?

So the tape ended up like the bootleg version. We let Glyn Johns remix it and we didn't want to know, we just left it to him and said, "Here, do it." It's the first time since the first album we didn't have anything to . . . we just said, "Do it." Glyn Johns did it, none of us could be bothered going in and Paul . . . nobody called anybody about it. The tapes were left there, and we got an acetate each, and we'd call each other and say, "Well, what do you think? Oh, let it out." We were going to let it out with a really shitty condition, disgusted. And I wanted . . . I didn't care, I thought it was good to go out to show people what had happened to us. Like this is where we're at now, we couldn't get—we can't get it together and don't play together anymore. Leave us alone [*laugh*]. Glyn Johns did a terrible job on it, cause he's got no idea, etc. Never mind. But he hasn't, really. And so the bootleg version is what it was like. Paul was probably thinking, "Well, I'm not going to fucking work on it." It was twenty-nine hours of tape, it was like a movie. I mean just so much tape. Ten, twenty takes of everything, because we're rehearsing and taking everything. Nobody could face looking at it.

So when Spector came around, it was like, "Well, alright, if you want to work with us [*laugh*], go and do your audition, man." And he worked like a pig on it. He'd always wanted to work with the Beatles and he was given the *shittiest* load of badly recorded shit—and with a lousy feeling to it—ever. And he made *something* out of it. It wasn't fantastic, but I heard it, I didn't puke. I was so relieved after six months of this black cloud hanging over, [that] this was going to go out. I thought it would be good to go out, the shitty version, because it would break the Beatles, it would break the myth. That's us with no trousers on and no glossy paint over the cover and no sort of hype. "This is what we're like with our trousers off. So would you please end the game now?" But that didn't happen, and we ended up doing *Abbey Road* quickly and putting out something slick to preserve the myth.

Why?

To preserve the myth.

That was Paul . . .

It's not like that. If it's suggested, I will go along. I'm *weak* as well as strong. I wasn't going to fight for *Let It Be*. Because I really couldn't stand it.

When 'Let It Be' was finally going to be released, Paul at that point wanted to release his solo album?

Oh, yeah. I don't quite . . . it's so many clashes. It did come out at the same time or something, didn't it?

Yeah.

I think he wanted to show he *was* the Beatles.

By bringing out 'McCartney'?

I think so.

Were you surprised when you heard it? At what he had done?

Yeah, I was surprised it was so poor. I expected just a little more, because if Paul and I are sort of disagreeing and I feel weak, I think he must feel strong. That's in an argument. Not that we've had much physical argument, I mean when we're talking—but you expect the opposition so-called. So I was just surprised. And I was glad, too [*laugh*]. I suddenly got it all in perspective.

What do you think Paul will think of your new album?

I think it'll probably scare him into doing something decent, and then he'll scare me into doing something decent, and I'll scare him like that. I think he's capable of great work. I think he *will* do it. I wish he wouldn't. I wish *nobody* would, Dylan or anybody. I mean in me heart of hearts I wish I was the only one in the world—or whatever it is. But I can't see him doing it twice.

I read something Derek [Taylor] wrote about cripples and other afflicted people coming up to you to be cured. What was that like?

Well, that was *our* version of what was happening. People were sort of touching us as we walked past, that kind of thing. Wherever we went we were supposed to be not normal and we were supposed to put up with all sorts of shit from lord mayors and their wives and be touched and pawed like *Hard Day's Night* only a million more times. At the American Embassy, the British Embassy in Washington, or wherever it was, some bloody animal cut Ringo's hair, in the middle of . . . I walked out of that. Swearing at all of them and I just left in the middle of it. But I've forgotten.

You tripped me off onto that. What was the question?

The cripples.

Oh, yeah. And wherever we went on tour, like in Britain or wherever we went, there's always a few seats laid aside for cripples and people in wheelchairs. Because we were famous, we were supposed to have people—sort of epileptics and whatever they are—in our dressing room all the time. We're supposed to be good. But you wanted to be alone, and you don't know what to say. They're usually saying, "I've got your record" or they can't speak or something. And they just want to touch . . . and it's always the *mother* or the nurse pushing them on you. They would just say hello and go away, they're pushing them at you like you're Christ or something, or as if there's some aura about you which will rub off on them. It just got to be like that. We got very *callous* about it. It was just dreadful. You'd open up every night, and instead of seeing kids there you'd just see a row full of cripples on the front. When we were running through, it seemed like [we were] just surrounded by cripples and blind people all the time. And when we'd go through corridors, everybody would be—they'd be all touching us. It got *horrifying*.

You must have been still fairly young and naïve at that point.

Yeah. Well, as naïve as *In His Own Write*.

Surely that must have made you think for a second.

About what?

About . . .

No, I mean we knew what the game was. The game is the same all . . .

Didn't it astound you at that point to see that you were supposed to be able to . . .

. . . that was a glib way of saying what was going on. It was sort of the "in" joke that we were supposed to cure them, it's the kind of thing that Derek would say. Because it's a cruel thing to say. We felt sorry for them. *Anybody* would. There's a kind of *embarrassment* when you're surrounded by blind, deaf and crippled people. There's only so much we could say, with the pressure on us to perform and things like that. But it just built up, it built up, the bigger we got, the more unreality we had to face, the more we were expected to do, until when you didn't shake hands with the mayor's wife, she starts abusing you and screaming or saying, "How dare they?" There's one of Derek's stories where we were asleep after the session, in the hotel somewhere in America, and this mayor's wife comes and says, "Get 'em up! I want to meet them." And Derek said, "I'm not going to wake them up." And she starts saying, "You get them up, I'll tell the press!" It was always that, they were always threatening what they would tell the press about us, the bad publicity if we didn't see their bloody daughter with braces on her teeth. And it was always the police chief's daughter and the lord mayor's, all the most *obnoxious* kids. Because they got the most obnoxious parents, we were forced to see all the time. And we had these people *thrust* on us. And [that was] the most humiliating experiences for me. Like sitting with the governor of the Bahamas because we were making *Help!* and being insulted by these fuckin' jumped-up middle-class bitches and bastards, who would be commenting on our work and our manners. And I was always *drunk*, like the typical—whatever it is—insulting them. I couldn't take it. It hurt me so, I would go insane, swearing at them and whatever. I'd always do something. I couldn't take it. It was awful. All that business was awful. It was a fuckin' humiliation. One has to completely humiliate oneself to be what the Beatles were, and *that's* what I resent. I *did* it, but I didn't know, I didn't foresee that, it just happened bit by bit til this complete craziness is surrounding you. And you're doing exactly what you don't want to do with people you can't *stand*—the people you *hated* when you were ten. And that's what I'm saying in this album, I'm saying, "I *remember* what it's all about now, you *fuckers, fuck you all.*" That's what I'm saying. "*Fuck you all. You don't get me twice!*"

Would you take it all back?

What?

Being a Beatle?

If I could be a fuckin' *fisherman*, I would! If I had the capabilities of being something other than I am, I *would*. It's no fun being an artist. You know what it's like writing, it isn't fun, it's *torture*. I read about Van Gogh or Beethoven, any of the fuckers. And I read an article the other day—"If they'd had psychiatrists, we wouldn't have had Gauguin's great pictures." And these fuckin' bastards, they're just sucking us to death. About all we can do is do it like fuckin' circus animals. I resent being an artist in that respect. I resent performing for fuckin' idiots who won't know—who don't know—anything. Cause they can't feel—I'm the one that's feeling, cause I'm the one expressing what they are trying to. They live vicariously through me and other artists. And we are the ones that—even with the boxers. When Oscar [Bonavena] comes in the ring, they're booing the shit out of him.[80] He only hit Clay once, they're all cheering him. That's what I resent. I'd sooner be in the audience, really, but I'm not *capable* of it. You know one of my big things is that I wish I was a fuckin' fisherman! I know it sounds silly, and I'd sooner be rich than poor and all the rest of that shit. But the pain, I'd sooner not be . . . I wish I was . . . ignorance is bliss or something. If you don't know, man, there's no pain. Oh, probably there is, but that's how I express it. It's *shit!*

What do you think the effect of the Beatles was on the history of Britain?

I don't know about on the history. The people who are in control

---

[80] A 1970 boxing match between Oscar Bonavena and Cassius Clay (who changed his name to Muhammad Ali). Clay won the match.

and in power and the class system and the whole bullshit bourgeois scene is exactly the same, except that there's a lot of fag fuckin' middle-class kids with long hair walking around London in trendy clothes. And Kenneth Tynan's making a fortune out of the word "fuck." But apart from that, nothing happened. But we all dressed up. The same bastards are in control, the same people are running everything. It's *exactly* the same! They *hyped* the kids. We've grown up a little, all of us, and there has been a change and we are a bit freer and all that, but it's the same game. Nothing's really changed. It's the *same*! History a bit and shit, they're doing exactly the same things, selling arms to South Africa, killing blacks on the street, people are living in fuckin' poverty with fuckin' rats crawling over 'em. It just makes you puke, and I woke up to that, too. That dream is over, it's just the same, only I'm thirty and a lot of people have got long hair, that's all.

YOKO: Very heavy, isn't it?

JOHN: That's what it is, man. Nothing happened, except that we grew up. We did our thing, just like they were telling us. "Well, well, you kids"—it's exactly the same. Most of the so-called "Now Generation" are getting a job and all that. Nothing changed, we're a *minority*. We're a minority like people like us always were. But maybe we're a slightly larger minority because of something or other.

YOKO: And what I respect about John's music is it's very real. You know how people tell children about Santa Claus and all that, and you know when you start not to believe in Santa Claus and all that shit, but the thing is, like George Harrison, the only thing that I object [to] is that he's still saying Santa Claus is there.

JOHN: But that—he—that's nothing . . .

YOKO: Cause he's just saying . . .

JOHN: Well that's a question of age or whatever, or the . . . his . . . he can't . . . he *believes* it, there's . . .

YOKO: It isn't that . . .

JOHN: It's not—it's not a conscious choice. He's twenty-five or something.[81]

YOKO: Well, it's just that the fact is . . .

JOHN: But it's no good—don't compare it with George . . .

YOKO: Oh, okay, I won't compare it with George, but he's . . .

JOHN: We're not talking about *that* anyway. We're talking about social revolution in England. No, I don't—I don't like—I don't want this—it's hard not to compare with George, even for us. But I don't want to be compared with *George*. Why should I be compared with George? What?

YOKO: You're right.

JOHN: You know, my music has nothing to do with George's.

Why do you think the impact of the Beatles was so much bigger in America than it was in England?

The same as American stars are so much bigger in England, I suppose. I don't know. Cause it's—

Greener grass?

Grass is greener. And we really were professional by the time we got here. We learned the whole game. When we arrived here, we knew how to handle press. The British press are the toughest in the world—we could handle anything. We were alright. I know on the plane over I was thinking, "Oh, we won't make it," or I said it on a film somewhere. But we knew. We would wipe them out if we could just get a grip on you. We were new. When we got here you were all walking around in fuck-

---

[81] Harrison was twenty-seven at the time.

ing bermuda shorts with Boston crewcuts and stuff on your teeth. And now they're telling us that—Beatles are passé and this is like that, man. The chicks looked like fuckin' 1940s horses. There was no conception of dress or any of that jazz. I mean we just thought, "What an ugly race." It looked just disgustin'. And we thought how hip we were, but, of course, we weren't. It was just the five of us—us and Mick—were really the hip ones, the rest of England is just the same as it ever was. But you tend to get nationalistic. We used to really laugh at America, except for its music. It was the black music we dug. Over here, even the blacks were laughing at people like Chuck Berry and the blues singers. The blacks thought it wasn't sharp to dig the really funky black music. The whites only listened to Jan and Dean and all that. We felt like we were . . . we had . . . the message was, "Listen to this music." It was the same in Liverpool. We felt very exclusive and underground in Liverpool listening to Ritchie Valens[82] and Barrett Strong[83] and all those old-time records that nobody was listening to anywhere, except for Eric Burdon [of the Animals] in Newcastle and Mick Jagger in London. It was that lonely—it was fantastic. And we came over here and it was the same. Nobody was listening to rock & roll or to black music in America. And we felt as though we were . . . we thought we were coming to the land of its origin. But nobody wanted to know about it.

[82] Mexican–American rocker Ritchie Valens had three hits ("Come On, Let's Go," "Donna" and "La Bamba") before he died in a 1959 plane crash at the age of seventeen.

[83] Barrett Strong had one of Motown's earliest hits, 1961's "Money," an early cover by the Beatles.

Why did you make "Revolution"?

Which one?

Both.

Three of 'em. There's three.

Right. Starting with the single.

When George and Paul and all them were on holiday, I made "Revolution," which is on the LP, and "Revolution 9," I wanted to put it out as a single, but they said it wasn't good enough. They came home, I had it all prepared and they came back and said it wasn't good enough and we put out, what, "Hello, Goodbye" or some *shit*. No, we put— "Hey Jude," sorry, which was worthy. But we could have had both. I wanted to put out what I felt about revolution, I thought it was about time we fuckin' spoke about it, the same as I thought it was about time we stopped not answering about the Vietnamese war, on tour with Brian. We had to tell him, "We're going to talk about the war this time, we're not going to just waffle." And I wanted to say what I thought about revolution. I'd been thinking about it up in the hills in India. And I still had this "God will save us" feeling about it. "It's going to be alright." But even now I'm saying, "Hold on, John, it's going to be alright."[84] Otherwise, I won't hold on. But that's why I did it, I wanted to say my piece about revolution. I wanted to tell *you* or whoever listens and communicate and say, "What do you say? This is what I say." And that's why I say on one version, about violence, "in or out?" because I wasn't sure. But the version we put out said, "Count me out," I think.[85] Because I

---

[84] Referring to "Hold On" on *John Lennon/Plastic Ono Band*.

[85] Lyric is "But when you talk about destruction/Don't you know that you can count me out."

don't fancy a violent revolution happening all over. I don't want to die. But I'm beginning to think that what else can happen. It seems inevitable.

The violent revolution?

Yeah. And the "Revolution 9" was an unconscious picture of what I actually think will happen when it happens. That was just like a drawing of revolution. Because arbitrarily, I was making . . . all the thing was made with loops. I had about thirty loops going, I fed them onto one basic track. I was getting like Beethoven and I'd go upstairs, chopping it up and making it backwards and things like that to get sound effects. And one thing was an engineer's testing [tape], where they'd come on talking and say [*in a robotic voice*], "This is EMI test series number nine." So I just cut up whatever he said, and I had "number nine." "Nine" is—I don't know, it turned out to be my birthday and me lucky number and everything, but I didn't realize it. It was just so funny, the voice went, "number nine." It was like a *joke*, bringing "number nine" in all the time. That's all it was.

YOKO: It turns out to be the highest number in the, one, two, etc. up to nine.

JOHN: Nine, yeah, it's the . . . it's all . . . many symbolic things about it, but it just happened. It was an engineer's tape and I was just using all the bits to make a montage. But I really wanted that out. Never mind. So that's how I feel. And I know the Chairman Mao bit, I always feel a bit strange about, cause I thought that if they're going to get hurt, the idea was, don't aggravate the pig by waving the red flag in his face. I really thought that—that love would save us all, but now I'm wearing a Chairman Mao badge, so that's where it's at. I'm just beginning to think he's doing a good job.

YOKO: He is.

JOHN: He seems to be. I would never know until I went to China. I'm not going to be like that. I'm not like that. I just was always interested enough to sing about him. But I just wondered what the kids were doing that were actually Maoists. I wonder what their motive was or what was *really* going on. And I thought, If they wanted revolution, if they really want to be subtle, what's the point of saying, "Well I'm a Maoist, and why don't you shoot me down?" I thought that was not a very clever way of getting what they wanted.

You don't really believe that we're headed for a violent revolution?

I don't know. I've got no more conception than you. I can't see— *eventually,* it'll happen. It *has* to happen. What else can happen? It might happen now, or it might happen in fifty or a hundred years, but it's like . . .

The problem is a violent revolution now would really just be the end of the world.

Not necessarily. They say that every time, but I don't really believe it. If it is, *okay*. I'm back to where I was when I was seventeen. At seventeen, I used to think, Well, I wish a fuckin' earthquake or a revolution would happen, just to go out and steal and do what the blacks are doing now. If I was black, I'd be all for it. And if I was seventeen, I'd be all for it, too, cause what have you got to lose? And now I've got nothing to lose. I don't want to die and I don't want to be hurt physically, but fuck, man, if they blow the world up, *fuck it!* We're all out of our pain then. *Forget it! No more problems!*

But you sing, "Hold on, world."[86]

---

[86] A lyric from *Plastic Ono Band*'s "Hold On."

Yeah, I sing "Hold on, John," too, because I don't want to die. And I'm a coward. I'm not a coward, I don't want to die. I don't want to be hurt. And please don't hit me!

So you feel like holding on, it will be alright?

It's only going to be alright *now*, this moment, that's alright. The thing we forgot about the acid was—to live *now, this moment.* And hold on *now*! We might have a cup of tea, or we might get a moment's happiness any minute now. So that's what it's all about. Just moment by moment. That's how we're living now. But *really* living like that. Cherishing each day and *dreading* it too.

YOKO: [*laugh*]

JOHN: It might be your last. I mean it sounds funny, but you might get run over by a car. Although I'm really beginning to *cherish* it when I'm cherishing it.

YOKO: That's true.

I like the philosophy of "Hold On," because there really is nothing else to do.

Yeah, just hold on day to day.

Let's talk about more tracks from the album, like "Isolation" and "Hold On."

"Isolation" and "Hold On John," they're the rough remixes. I just remixed them that night on seven-and-a-half to take them home to see what else I was going to do with them.[87] And then I didn't really, I didn't even put them on to fifteen, so the quality is a bit [*hisses*]-y on 'em too. By the time I'd done everything, I started listening. I

---

[87] Seven-and-a-half [inches per second] refers to the speed the tape goes over the tape head; the slower the tape, the lower the quality.

found out it's better that, with "Instant Karma" and other things, you remix it right away that night. I'd known that before, but never followed it through. There's nothing like that re—usually the remix that you do [on] the day you do the session, because you know—there's a—it really—it worked on every one that I did like that. I just remixed them the same night, "Hold On John" and "Isolation" and—oh "I Found Out," but I did change it later, actually. Especially those two.

Did you put in "fucking" deliberately on "Working Class Hero"?

No, I put it in because it does fit. I didn't even realize there was *two* in til somebody pointed it out. And actually when I sang it, I missed a bloody verse. I had to edit it in. But you do say "fucking crazy," don't you? That's how I speak. I was very near to it many times in the past, but I would deliberately not put it in, which is the *real* hypocrisy, the *real* stupidity. I would deliberately *not* say things, because it might upset somebody, or whatever I was frightened of.

"Happiness Is a Warm Gun" is a nice song.

Oh, yeah, I like that one of me best, I forgot about that.

A weird one.

What?

That was a weird one.

Oh, I love that, you know?

Why?

Because I think it's a [*laugh*] beautiful song. I just like all the different things that are happening in it. That was like "God." I put together three sections of different songs. But it was meant to be like—I don't know, it seemed to run through all the different kinds of rock music. It wasn't about H at all.

"Happiness Is a Warm Gun"?

No. It wasn't. It was never—like all the ones that really—like LSD, the "Lucy in the Sky," which I swear to God or swear to Mao, or anybody you like, I'd no intention. "Happiness Is a Warm Gun" is the same. George Martin had a fuckin' book on guns, or he told me about it—I can't remember—I think he showed me a cover of a magazine that said, "Happiness Is a Warm Gun." It was a gun magazine. I just thought it was a fantastic, insane thing to say. A warm gun means you just shot something [*laugh*].

On "Lucy in the Sky," when did you realize that the initials spelled LSD?

Only after I read it—or somebody told me, like you coming up. I didn't even see it on the label, I didn't look at the initials. I never play things backwards, I just listened to it as I made it. There will be things on this one, if you fiddle about with it, but I don't know what they are. Every time after, I would look at titles, see what it said, but it never said anything.

You said to me, 'Sgt. Pepper's' was the one, that was the album.

It was a peak, and Paul and I definitely were working together, especially on "A Day in the Life." That was a real . . . the way we wrote a lot of the time was he'd write the good bit that was easy, like "I read the news today, oh boy"—or whatever it was, or "Day Tripper," anything like that. And then when you got stuck, instead of carrying on—whenever it got hard—you'd just drop in and meet each other and I'd sing half and he'd be inspired to write the next bit and vice versa. And then he came up with that. And he was a bit shy about it, cause I think he thought, "Well, it's a good song" [and] sometimes we wouldn't let each other interfere with a song either. Cause you tend to be a bit lax with somebody else's stuff—you experiment a bit. We were doing it in his room with the piano, and he's saying, "Would you—should we do this?" I said, "Yeah, let's do that." And that's how it happened.

I always kept saying I prefer the double album [the "White Album"], cause *my* music is better on the double album. I don't care about the whole concept of *Pepper*. It might be better, but the *music* is better for me on the double album, because I'm being meself on it. I'm doing it how I like it. It's as simple as this album [*Plastic Ono Band*], my stuff on the double album. Like "I'm So Tired" and all that, it's just the guitar. I felt more at ease with *that* than the production. I don't like productions so much, but *Pepper* was a peak, alright.

YOKO: In a way, the thing is, people . . .

JOHN: Hello.

YOKO: Yes. People say something like, "Oh, that's the peak," and I'm just so amazed. I see groups we thought that do well, John's done all that Beatles stuff and everything. But this *new* album of John's is a *real* peak that's higher than any other thing that he has done.

JOHN: Thank you, dear.

Do you think it is?

Yeah, sure. I think it's, you know, "Sgt. Lennon."

YOKO: It's a real revolution.

JOHN: I don't really know how it'll sink in, or where it'll lie, in the spectrum of rock & roll and the generation and all the rest of it. But I know what it is. It's something else, and it's another door . . .

YOKO: That you don't even know yet, or realize it.

JOHN: . . . sneakingly aware of but not fully . . .

YOKO: No.

JOHN: . . . until it's all over, like anybody else. No, we didn't know really what *Pepper* was going to do or what anything was going to do. I have a feeling, but I don't know whether it's going to settle down in a minority. It could do that, because in one way it's terribly uncommercial. It's so miserable in a way and heavy, but it's *reality*. I'm not going to veer away from it for anything.

YOKO: The thing is, the psychedelic age brought this thing about music with lots of decorative sounds, *so* decorative. And I think George probably . . .

JOHN: Oh, Yoko, you keep talking about George.

YOKO: I was thinking, like Tom Jones, is like . . .

Getting back to it.

YOKO: Tom Jones is like medium without message. John's stuff is like— instead of medium is the message, which was the psychedelic age, medium the message. *He's* like the *message* is the medium. And it's *really* the message. Because it was so important, he didn't need any decorative sound, or decorativeness about it. That's why in some songs it seems like the accompaniment is simple or something. But it was like an urgent message, I feel.

JOHN: [*like a radio announcer*] Thank you and good night.

How did you first get in touch with Allen Klein?

I got various messages through various people like from Robert Fraser and people like that that: "Allen Klein would like to talk to you." I knew who he was, and I heard about him over the years. The first time I heard about him was when he said, one day he'd have the Beatles. But he offered Brian this good deal, which in retrospect hearing about it, Brian probably should have done at the time. This was years ago, but that's when I first heard about him. I had heard all these dreadful rumors about him, but I could never coordinate it with why the Stones seemed to be going on and on with him. Nobody ever said a word and Mick's not the type to just clam up. So "it must be a lie." But still, when I heard he wanted to see me, I thought—I got nervous. Because I know when some businessman wants to see me, it's going to be business, and business makes me nervous. I finally got the message from Mick, and Allen had set up a deal that Mick and us nearly went into an Apple together a few years back. We had big meetings discussing about the studios and all that, but it never happened. And Allen wanted to come in that way. It was after Brian [died], but it didn't happen like that. All these approaches were coming from all over the place. I met him at the *Rock and Roll Circus*, which has never been seen, John and Yoko performing together for the first time with a crazy violinist and Keith on bass and all that.[88] I'll always regret that. And I met him there, but I didn't know what to make of him, just shook hands. [*To Yoko*] And then what happened?

YOKO: Then one day we finally decided to meet him. Remember?

JOHN: Yeah, we just sort of decided to meet him. But did we call him or did we accept *his* call? He called me once, I never accepted the call in the house, I think in Kenwood. I didn't take it, I was too nervous. I don't like talking to strangers as it is, but strangers want to talk about

---

[88] The Rolling Stones' *Rock and Roll Circus* was a never-completed TV show, filmed on December 11, 1968, that mocked variety shows and featured the Rolling Stones playing with a number of other artists including John Lennon and Yoko Ono. A video and CD of the show was finally released in 1996.

reality, so I didn't accept the call. And then finally I did accept the call or did I put a call through to him? He'll tell you. He knows the lyrics to every fuckin' song you'd ever imagine from the Twenties on! I was with him eating last night, I was just singing a few things, because she thinks I know every song that—I know millions of songs, I'm like a jukebox of thousands upon millions of chords and stuff. But he not only knows it, he knows every fuckin' word, not just the chorus, like— oh, I can't think of a one now, like "Smoke Gets in Your Eyes" or whatever, but every fuckin' word. He's got memory like that. But then we met and it was very traumatic.

In what way?

JOHN: Well, cause we were both very nervous. He was nervous as shit, and I was nervous as shit, and Yoko was nervous as him. We met at the Dorchester, we went up to his room and I—

YOKO: We were so nervous—

JOHN: I just went in and he was sitting there all nervous, and he was all alone. He didn't have any of his helpers around, because he didn't want to do anything like that. But he was very nervous, you could see it in his face. So I felt better. But I don't know, he knows exactly what we said and what we did from—so if you ever want to get that story—I don't remember, she knows—she's got a pretty good memory. We talked to him a few hours—and we decided that night . . .

YOKO: It happened very quickly.

JOHN: . . . he was *it*.

What made you decide that?

Because he not only knew my work and the lyrics that I'd written, understood 'em, and from *way* back. If he knew what I was saying and followed me work, then that was pretty damn good for me, because it's hard to see me, John Lennon, in amongst all that. And he talked sense about what had happened. He just said what was going on. And I just knew.

Like what?

YOKO: Very intelligent guy.

JOHN: He's an intelligent guy, he told me all that was happening with the Beatles, my relationship with Paul and George and Ringo. He knew every damn thing about us. The same as he knows everything about the Stones. He's a *fuckin'* sharp man. There's things he doesn't know, but when it comes to that kind of business, he knows. And anybody that knew me that well, without ever having met me, had to be a guy that I could let look after me. He knew how to handle me, to look after me. I let him handle the business. So I wrote to Sir Joe [Lockwood] that night.[89] We were so pleased, I said, "Okay, we'll write to Sir Joe." I said, "I don't care what the others say, you can handle me." Yoko always was my advisor, so's I wouldn't go into any Maharishis anymore. So whether it was Derek or people coming to take over Apple when we were running at Wigmore Street and interviewing people for all that, and Yoko would sit behind me and advise—I'd play me games and she'd tell me what they were doing when I blinked and how they were in her opinion, because she wasn't as stupid as me, or emotional. It was like Janov's book in a way, We thought, "Well . . . only before, when the Beatles were against the world did I have the cooperation of a good mind like Paul's." It was us against them. But for the last few years I've been on me own. But Yoko was intelligent and . . .

So you wrote Lockwood?

[89] Sir Joseph Lockwood was chairman of EMI from 1954 to 1974.

I wrote Lockwood, saying "Dear Sir Joe"—cause he was always such a bastard—"from now on Allen Klein handles all my stuff." He's got it framed somewhere. And I posted it that night. Allen couldn't believe . . . he was—[*gasp*]—so excited [*laugh*]. "At last, at last." He was trying not to push, he was trying . . .

You made a one-year deal.

Then, I don't know. I just was saying, "You can handle me, and I'll tell the others you seem alright and you can come and meet George and everything and Paul and all them." And . . .

So Ringo was happy to go along?

No, they didn't do what I wanted. I had to present a case, and Allen had to present—talk to them himself. But I just said, listen—and Eastman was there too—I just told them what I thought of him.[90] And of course I promoted him in the—in the fashion of which I will—you see me promoting something, or talking about something. I was enthusiastic about him and I was relieved because I met a lot of people including Lord Beeching, who's one of the top people in Britain and all that. And though he didn't want to take the job, Paul had told me, "Go and see Lord Beeching." So I went. I mean I'm a good boy, man. And I saw Lord Beeching and he was no help at all and he didn't look nice. I mean, he was alright.

YOKO: Yeah.

JOHN: He was alright, and everybody I interviewed for the . . . while Paul was in America getting Eastman, I was interviewing all these top

[90] Paul meantime had married American photographer Linda Eastman, whose father, Lee, and brother, John, were music business lawyers who also wanted to manage the Beatle affairs.

so-called."people." And they were animals. Allen was a human being. The same as Brian was a human being. It was the same thing with Brian in the early days. It was assessment, and I make a lot of mistakes character-wise. But now and then I make a . . . I don't make . . . I make a good one, and Allen's one, Yoko's another one, Brian was one. And so I'm closer to him than anybody else, outside of Yoko.

How did the rest of the Beatles react?

I don't remember. They were nervous like me because this terrible man who had got the Rolling Stones and said that he was going to get the Beatles years ago and all that, and "You don't know what's going on." I don't know what we did next.

YOKO: Somebody said, "Please, let's see Allen and Eastman *together* and see how it is."

JOHN: Yeah. But what did I say to George then? Did I ring them or something? I suppose I rung them.

YOKO: No, we were going to Apple with them so we met George there.

JOHN: But did I say, "This is Allen Klein and we met him *last* night"? I know that I said that he was okay and you should meet and all that. And then we got Paul because John Eastman had already been in. We almost signed ourselves over to the Eastmans at one time. When Paul presented me with John Eastman, I thought . . . when you're not presented with a *real* alternative, you take whatever's going. I would say "Yes, let's do *Let It Be*," or "Yeah, there's no real . . ."—and I can't think of anything, I have no thing to produce, I will go along. And we almost went away with Eastman, but then Eastman made the mistake of sending his son over and not coming over himself to look after the Beatles. Playing it a bit cool. So finally, when we got near the point and Allen came in, they panicked. I was still open, I would have taken Eastman if he'd turned out [to be] something other than he was. But we arranged to see Eastman and Klein together, in a hotel where one of them was staying. And for the four Beatles and Yoko to go and see them both. We hadn't been in there more than a few minutes when Eastman was having like an epileptic fit and screaming at Allen, that he was the lowest scum on earth and calling him all sorts of names. And Allen was sitting there taking it. Because he was just taking it, this guy was abusing him with class snobbery. And we all know Eastman's name is Epstein. And the rest of it. That's the kind of people they are. But Paul fell for that bullshit because he's got Picassos hanging on the wall, and because he's got some kind of East Coast suit. Form and not substance. And that's McCartney.

YOKO: I can't believe he fell for it.

JOHN: We were all still not sure and they brought in this fucking fellow, and he had an epileptic fit. We had thought it was one in a million but that was enough for me. Soon as he started nailing him on his taste, Paul was getting in little digs about Allen's dress and all that—just go and look at Paul's dress or his father or anything—what the fuck does he think he is! Him talking about dress! And *appearances*, man. Fucking hell. And so that was it, we said "*fuck it!*" I wouldn't let [Eastman] near me. I wouldn't let a fuckin' *animal* like that near me who has a *mind* like that. Who *despises me* too! Despises me because of what I am! Of what I look like! These people like Eastman and people like him think that I'm an idiot. And Dick James and all of them. They really can't see me.

YOKO: No, no.

JOHN: And they think I'm some kind of guy who got struck lucky, a pal of Paul's or something. They're so fuckin' *stupid*, they don't know. The reason Allen knew was cause he knew who I was. He wasn't going on what a pretty face I'd got. Eastman *blew* it, man, and then he went on to do it *again*. Where did he do it? Next time he did it in the Apple office, but he keeps coming to me and saying, "Try and hold this *madness* down," this *insanity* that kept coming out. And the son's so uptight you can hardly . . . the whole family's like that, they're so uptight, there must be a maniac scene there!

YOKO: Can you imagine what he did was . . .

JOHN: He kept going up to me saying, "I can't tell you how much I admire you." Gortikov from Capitol does that too.[91] They're full of praise, unlike the immigration officer, which we won't mention cause we're *here* so I can't . . . "Don't be afraid of me, I can't tell you how much I've admired your work, John"—really thinking, "Just give me the copyrights to 'Yesterday,'" and really thinking, "'Yesterday''s all that counts." And I'm just watching this, and thinking, "It's happening to me" and "Thank you very much" and all that. [*To Yoko*] What was the second epileptic fit, because I want *this* out! What was the second time he *blew* it?

YOKO: In Apple or something.

JOHN: I don't know, he did it in front of everybody in Apple. This was supposed to be the guy who was taking over the multimillion-dollar corporation and who was going to be slick and who was sort of intimating that Allen's Broadway offices [weren't nice enough], Paul was saying, as if that meant any fuckin' difference. Where Eastman's was in the good section of town. "Oh boy, man, that's where it's at, and Eastman's office has got class!" I don't care if this is fuckin' red, white and blue! I don't care what Allen dresses like! He's a *human being*, man.

91 Stanley E. Gortikov, the former chairman of Capitol Records.

YOKO: Paul said, *you know*, "Allen's office is in Broadway, Yoko."

JOHN: And I'm thinking, "Well what does that . . . maybe good taste counts [*laugh*]."

YOKO: And then he said that . . .

JOHN: But Eastman went around blowing at everybody . . . you know what he does, he writes letters to everybody saying, "Don't you *dare*"— and he's got no right . . . he's completely mad!

Still?

Sure, he's still doing it!

So you said no to Eastman. What did Paul do?

The more we said "No," the more he said "Yes." It's just like that. I don't know. We're still talking, and Eastman went mad and started shouting and all that. And I don't know what Paul was thinking in the room, I mean his heart must've sunk. I think it's cause he's in the family.

YOKO: They were saying that they don't even want to come to meetings where Allen is.

JOHN: Eastman was refusing to *meet* Allen, saying "I will not meet such a low rat!" What the *fuck* has Klein done! He never done a fuckin' thing! All this income tax shit, he'd been cleared, and even if he *hadn't*, so what the *fuck*, all these fuckin' wolves and sharks, how *dare* they call him for being what he is. How *dare* they insult anybody like that! They're *fuckin' bastards*, they're—Eastman's a WASP Jew, man! And that's the worst kind of Jew on earth, that's the worst kind of WASP too—he's a WASP Jew, can you imagine it!

YOKO: And can you imagine what they did? Like to meet with Allen in New York . . .

JOHN: They refused to meet him . . .

YOKO: . . . they invited . . . they . . .

JOHN: . . . I said, you don't meet anybody—I don't talk to anybody unless I come along with Allen. They said, "Come on, John, I want to meet you alone."

YOKO: Right.

JOHN: I said, "I don't see any of you without Allen with me!"

YOKO: We don't want to be in the same room with . . .

JOHN: With Allen.

YOKO: . . . with that guy. But the thing is, what he did finally, when they met, they invited Allen to the Harvard Club, can you imagine that? Just to show . . .

JOHN: And when Eastman finally was signing something, God knows what it was, he made us all come. There was something, Allen will tell you the details if he wants to talk about it. I had to jump over a fence and get Paul's signature for something, which finally secured us our position. And he really started insulting me then.

Who?

Eastman. He knew the game was over.

At the Harvard Club?

No, it was the equivalent in London. The three of us had to go there to get his final approval on Paul's signature which we'd got, but he went through every line, pretending . . . he's an idiot, he doesn't know from Adam! He's living off the copyrights of some shit that he conned years ago! And he's initialing all these things just to slow us down, like an immigration officer, really putting us through it. And I'm . . . we're waiting there [thinking], "Sign it, you *fuckin'* idiot and let's get out," but he starts insulting me.

YOKO: Um.

JOHN: What was he saying? [Yoko] said, "Will you please stop insulting my husband." He had his few lawyers with him, and this sort of fuckin' phony club, and he's going, "You're stupid! Tell him how stupid it is signing with this guy! Tell him how stupid it is!" And she was saying, "Don't call my husband stupid." I wasn't saying anything but "Just sign it and just give me the signature, just put your initials on it, *Epstein*," I was thinking, "Let's get out of here. And we'll *wrap* you up." And that's what we did! You can't believe it, man! The guy had epileptic fits, and then expected to run the company!

And Allen even offered John Eastman to be the *lawyer* for the deals we were making with Northern Songs, but they screwed him deliberately. They were screwing everything Allen did. It fucked all the Northern Songs deal and all that, but we still came out with all the money. They couldn't outmaneuver him. Klein not only knew our characters and what the relationship between the group was, the same way he knows Creedence Clearwater, he knows his business, he knows *who's who* in the group, what you have to do to get things done! And also he knew about every fuckin' contract and paper we'd ever had! He understood. And Eastman was making judgments and saying things to Paul based on something that he'd never *seen*! It was a wipeout, you can't imagine! The real story will never come out because Allen knows every detail, and he remembers everything we've said.

YOKO: The first approach was, well, he knew I went to Sarah Lawrence.

JOHN: Oh yeah.

YOKO: He was saying "Kafka-esque" and all that, and . . .

JOHN: Talking in those . . .

YOKO: . . . talking in a very "in" way. "We're middle class, aren't we," kind of . . .

JOHN: And Allen said, "Who's Kafka [*laugh*]?"

YOKO: [*Laugh*] But the point is, he doesn't know that I was a Sarah Lawrence dropout because I was sick and tired of that middle-class scene, and I married a *working-class hero*. It's that, isn't it? And John Eastman is a law student or something that comes to Sarah Lawrence. I would never date one of those uptight WASPy [*laugh*] . . .

JOHN: Yeah, with the veins stickin' out of my neck . . .

YOKO: . . . WASPy, you know—and if he's a true aristocrat—from a WASP class, he's not going to invite Allen to Harvard Club, he's going to make sure that he will invite Allen to somewhere that Allen would enjoy.

JOHN: Second-generation idiots. That's what he is.

YOKO: That's the kind of scummy thing I don't like.

So what was it like with Paul then?

Well, Paul was getting more and more uptight, til then Paul wouldn't speak to us without his . . . he told us, you speak to my lawyer.

When did you first start having unpleasant words with Paul over that?

We never had unpleasant words.

YOKO: No, not really.

JOHN: It never got to a talking thing, you see.

YOKO: No.

JOHN: It just got that Paul one day said, "Speak to my lawyer, I don't want to speak about business anymore." Which meant "I'm gonna drag my feet." The whole Northern thing was going on, and we were trying to save our fuckin' stuff! And he was playing hard to get, like a *fucking chick*! Because he hadn't thought of it. It was a pure ego game. And I got into the ego thing, of course, but I was really fighting for what I believed was our money and our fuckin' business! It wasn't just cause I'd found Allen, I would've dropped Allen if Eastman had been something. But he was a fuckin' *animal*! And a fuckin' stupid middle-class pig who didn't know from Adam about *nothin'* and thought he could con me with fuckin' talking about Kafka! And *shit*, Picasso . . .

YOKO: And de Kooning, Willem de Kooning.

JOHN: De Kooning, man, I shit on the *fuckin'* lot of 'em! Heh-heh. [*Pause*] Yeah. Heh-heh.

YOKO: I mean that was their level, de Kooning, you know, I would kick a de Kooning and burn it . . .

JOHN: I don't even know who the fuck they are, I just know it's something that somebody's got hung up on the wall that he thinks is an investment.

What was the state of the Beatles business at that point?

Chaos. Exactly what I said in ROLLING STONE, wasn't it? It all happens in the ROLLING STONE! But Steve Maltz—Allen said I must've got it from Steve Maltz, this accountant who we fired because we couldn't stand him, a young guy, who just sent me a letter one day saying, "You're in chaos. You're losing—this is so much a week going out of Apple." People are always saying, "You sold out the dream of Apple." People were robbing us and living on us for the tune of fuckin' eighteen or twenty thousand pounds a week [that] was rolling out of Apple like that, and nobody was doing anything about it. All our buddies that worked for us for fifty years, all just living and drinking and eating like fuckin' *Rome*, man! And I suddenly realized it! And I said it to you, "We're losing money at such a rate that we would have been broke, really broke." We didn't have anything in the bank, really, none of us did. Paul and I could have probably floated, but we would have just sunk in—we were sinking fast! It was just hell! It had to stop! When

Allen heard me say that—he read it in STONE—he came over right away, he said, now—soon as he realized that I knew what was going on, then he said, "Now I can get through." Until somebody knows they're in Shit Street, how can somebody come and get in? It's just like somebody coming up to me *now* and saying, "I want to help you with the business." I would say, "I've *got* somebody or I'm doing alright, Jack." But soon as [Allen] realized I *realized* what was going on, he came over.

How much money do you have now?

I'm not telling. Heh-heh-heh-heh. *Lots* more than I ever had before! Allen's got me more money, *real* money in the bank, than I've ever had in the whole period. And I've got money that I earned but eight or ten years of my fuckin' life, instead of all these Dick James Music Company and the whole . . .

How much were you making in that period?

I don't know. If Allen wants to talk about that, he'll talk about it to you, because I don't know. I just know it was *millions*. But Brian was no good businessman. He had a *flair* for presenting things, he was more *theatrical* than actual substance of business. And he was hyped a lot. He was advised by the gang of crooks, really. That's what's going on, and the battle's still going on to the Beatles' rights. The latest one is the Lew Grade thing—it's still going on. If you read *Cashbox*, you see what's happening. We put in a bill to Lew Grade for five million pounds.[92] And my songs have gone on Maclen Limited, not Northern Songs. They've been underpaying us for fucking years, Dick James, the whole lot of 'em, sold us out. And they still think we're like Tommy Steele[93] or

---

[92] In unpaid royalties.

[93] Britain's first homegrown rock & roll star in the 1950s.

some fuckin' product that none of them realize that just simply because of *Hard Day's Night* we got to wake up one day! And we're not the same as the last generation of stars or whatever they were fucking called.

How did it get down to Paul telling Ringo he was going to get him someday?

I don't know. It happened. It didn't happen in front of me. I think it happened on the phone. I just knew that . . .

When Ringo was sent around to say, "Look, we don't want the album out" . . .

Oh yeah, that was it. Because we thought it was unfair even though it was Paul's first new album, that was alright, we weren't against him puttin' an album out. I mean I'd done it. And I didn't think it was any different, except for Paul sang, and mine happened to be *Toronto* because that happened to happen. If I hadn't gone to Toronto, I would have made an album probably. I was half hoping I would make single after single and until there was enough for an album *that* way, because I'm lazy. But anyway, there was nothing *against* Paul having an album out. There was an *atmosphere* about Eastman and Klein, but it's alright. It's *business*, we all profit from it. But we didn't want to put it out against *Let It Be*, it would have killed the sales. It's like in the old days we used to watch, if the Stones were coming out, we'd ask Brian, "Who's coming out?" You know? And he'd tell us who's coming out shortly, and we'd say, "Well, we'll put it out now." We could always beat everyone, but what's the point of losing sales to somebody else? We'd time it! Mick timed it! We never came out together. Nobody ever . . . we're not that idiot . . .with Elvis, we miss everyone. I would miss Tom Jones, anybody *now!* I don't want to fight in the charts! I want to get in while the going's good. It would have killed . . . it was just an ego game! It would have killed *Let It Be*. Let *Let It Be* breathe!

But Paul didn't want to.

No!

So . . .

I can't remember, he just insisted on putting it out. We asked Ringo to go and talk to him because the real fighting had been going on between me and Paul, and because Eastman and Klein and we were on the opposite ends about *that*. So Ringo had not taken sides, and he'd always been straight about it, and we thought Ringo would be able to talk *fairly*. If Ringo agreed that it was *unfair*, it was unfair, it was like that! Paul wanted—even at one time he wanted a fuckin' extra vote on our voting trust, but that was the same as like the four of us at a table, but Paul has *two votes*! Something was going on that Paul *thought* he was the fuckin' Beatles! And he *never fucking* was! *Never, never. None of* us were the fucking Beatles! Four of us were!

YOKO: Aren't you hungry?

JOHN: Yeah.

YOKO: Shall we just go into some place and just have a bite or something?

JOHN: Yeah. Well, we can't, [Jann has] got to go somewhere and we're taping. Let's finish this . . .

YOKO: Okay.

JOHN: . . . and then we can go and eat, and at the hotel you got all them people.

So that was it. Ringo went and asked him and he attacked Ringo and threatened him and everything. And that was the kibosh for Ringo. I don't know what the situation is now.

Allen says that you all are going to get together in a few months.

I think we have to have a meeting shortly, because we all agreed to meet sometime in February to see where we are financially. It's *business*. We have to.

Do you think you all will ever record again?

No. *Not a chance.* I wouldn't record with *anyone* again. I record with Yoko, but I'm not going to record with another egomaniac. There's only room for one on an album nowadays, and so there's no point. There's just no point at all. At one time there was a reason to do it, but there's no reason to do it anymore. I had a *group*, I was the *singer* and the *leader*. I met Paul, and I made a decision whether to—and he made a decision too—whether to have him in the group or not. Was it better to have a guy who was better than the people I had—obviously—or not? To make the group stronger or to let me be stronger? That decision was to let Paul in to make the *group* stronger. Then from that, Paul introduced me to George, and Paul and I had to make the decision—or I had to make the decision—whether to let George in. And I listened to him play and said, "Play raunchy," or whatever the old story is, and I let him in. I said okay, "You come in," and that was the—that was the three of us then. And then the rest of the group was thrown out gradually. It just happened like that. Instead of going for an individual thing, we went for the strongest format. And for equals. But George is ten years younger than me, or some shit like that.[94] I couldn't be bothered with him when he first came round. He

---

[94] In actuality, George was only three years younger than John, but when they first started playing together in the Quarrymen, George was fifteen and John was eighteen.

used to follow me around like a bloody kid, hanging around all the time. It took me years to come round to him, to start considering him as an equal or anything. He was a kid who played guitar. And he was a friend of Paul's and made it all easier. Then we had all sorts of different drummers over time. Cause they—people who owned drum kits were far and few between. It was an expensive item. And they were usually idiots. And then we ended up—we got Pete Best just because we needed a drummer the next day to go to Hamburg. We'd passed the audition on our own with a stray drummer. And there's other myths about Pete Best was the Beatles or Stuart Sutcliffe was the Beatles, his mother's writing [that] in England.

You're the Beatles.

No, *I'm* not the Beatles, I'm *me*. But nobody's the Beatles. Paul isn't the Beatles. And Brian Epstein isn't the Beatles, neither is Dick James. The Beatles are the Beatles and separately they're separate. Nobody's the Beatles. How could they be? We all had our roles to play. [pause] George was a separate individual singer with his own group as well before he came in with us. He had the Rebels.

You say now on the record, "I don't believe in the Beatles."

Yeah. I don't believe in the Beatles, that's all.

What were the Beatles?

I don't believe in the Beatles myth. I don't believe in the Beatles— there's no other way of saying it, is there? I don't *believe* in them, whatever they were supposed to be in everybody's head, and including our own for a period. It was a dream. That's all. I don't believe in the dream anymore. But I made me mind up not to talk about all that shit. I'm sick of it. I'd like to talk about the album, which I was going to do and say to you, "Look, Jann, I don't want to talk about all that Beatles splitting up," because it not only hurts me, but it always ends up look-ing like I'm blabbing off and just attacking people. I don't want it!

How would you assess George's talents?

I don't want to assess him. George has not done his best work yet. His talents have developed over the years, and he was working with two fucking brilliant songwriters and he learned a lot from us. And I wouldn't have minded being George, the invisible man, and learning what he learned. And maybe it was hard sometimes for him, because Paul and I are such egomaniacs, but that's the game. So is George—just give him a chance, and he'll be the same. The best thing he's done is "Within You Without You," still for me. I can't assess his talents. He's not the kind of person I would buy the records of. But I don't want to *say* this about him. It will hurt him. I don't want to hurt his feelings. But just personally, I think it's nothing. "Something" was a nice tune, but it doesn't *mean* anything to me. I'm talking about not just rock & roll, just the *universe* or whatever. I don't consider my talents fantastic compared with the fuckin' universe, but I consider George's less. As an artist I can only consider myself.

If you ask me what music I listen to, I'm not really interested in con-cepts and philosophies and not wallpaper, which most music is.

What music do you listen to today?

I don't. If you want the record bit, I mean since I've been listening to the radio here I like something or whatever it is called by Neil Young—[*half singing*] "Something special"[95]—and something by Elton John. A song by him. And a few things I've heard. But I couldn't—didn't find

---

[95] Lennon may have been referring to a track from Young's album, *After the Gold Rush*.

out who they were. On FM. Some really good sound, but then there's no—there's no follow through. There'll be a section of fantastic sound come over the radio and then you wait for the *conclusion* or the *concept* or something to finish it off, and then *nothing* happens, it just goes on. A jam session or whatever.

You've had a chance to listen to FM radio in New York. What have you heard?

Yeah. "My Sweet Lord." Every time I put the radio on it's "Oh my Lord"—I'm beginning to think there must be a God! I knew there wasn't when "Hare Krishna" never made it on the polls with their own record, that really got me suspicious. We used to say to them, "You might get Number One" and they'd say, "Higher than that."

What do we hear? It's interesting to hear Van Morrison. He seems to be doing nice stuff—sort of 1960s black music—he is one of them that became an American like Eric Burdon. I just never have time for a whole album. I only heard Neil Young twice—you can pick him out a mile away, the whole style. He writes some nice songs. I'm not stuck on Sweet Baby [James Taylor]—I'm getting to like him more hearing him on the radio, but I was never struck by his stuff. I like Creedence Clearwater. They make beautiful Clearwater music—they make good rock & roll music. You see it's difficult when you ask me what I like, there's lots of stuff I've heard that I think is fantastic on the radio here, but I haven't caught who they are half the time.

But I'm interested in more things with a worldwide—I'm interested in what's it called, something that means something for *everyone*, not just for a few *kids* listening to wallpaper. I'm just as interested in poetry or whatever or art or anything. And always *have* been. That's been my *hangup*, continually trying to be *Shakespeare* or whatever it is. That's what I'm doing, I'm not pissing about. I consider I'm up against *them*, I'm not competing meself against Elvis.

YOKO: Or multiple artists.

JOHN: Or multiple artists, whatever. I'm in the game of *all* those things. Of *concept* and *philosophy* and *ways* of *life* and *whole movements* in *history*. I'm not interested in good guitarists. Just like Van Gogh was or any other of those fucking people, they're no more nor less than I am or Yoko is. They're no more, no less, they were just living those days. I'm interested in producing—expressing myself, like they expressed it, that will mean something to people in any country, in any language, and at any time in history. And rock just happens to be the media which I was born into, that's all. It was the one. It's like those people picked up paint brushes, Van Gogh probably wanted to be Renoir or whoever went before him. And I wanted to be Elvis or whatever the shit it is. But to me it's *art*.

When did you realize that what you were doing really transcended . . .

Listen, people like me are aware of their genius so-called at ten, eight, nine. I *always* thought I was—why has nobody discovered me? In school, can't they see that I'm cleverer than anybody in this school? That the teachers are stupid too? That all they had was information, which I didn't need, to give me? I didn't become aware of it in the *Beatle* thing. I got fuckin' *lost* in that, like being at high school or something. I used to say to my auntie, "You've thrown my fuckin' poetry out and you'll regret it when I'm famous!" And she threw the bastard stuff out. I never *forgave* her, for not treating me like a fuckin' genius or whatever I was when I was a child! It was *obvious* to me! Why didn't they put me in art school? Why didn't they train me? Why would they keep forcing me to be a fuckin' cowboy like the rest of them? I was different, I was *always different*! *Why* didn't anybody notice me? A couple of teachers would notice me, encourage me to be something or other, to draw or to paint, express meself. But most of the time they were trying to *beat* me into being a *fuckin'* dentist or a teacher! And then the fuckin' *fans* tried to beat me into being a fuckin' . . .

YOKO: Beatle.

JOHN: . . . Beatle or an Engelbert Humperdinck and the critics tried to beat me into being *Paul McCartney!* And all the rest of it!

YOKO: So you were very *deprived* in a way.

JOHN: But that's what makes me what I am! It comes out that people like me *have* to save themselves, because we get fucking *kicked!* Nobody says it! Zappa's there screaming, "Look at me, I'm a genius, for fuck's sake, what do I have to do to prove to you son-of-a-bitches what I can do and who I am and don't *dare* fuckin' criticize my *work* like that! You who don't know anything about it!" Fucking *bullshit!* I know what Zappa's going through! And a half! I'm just coming out of it now, just fuckin' hell, I've been in school again, I've had teachers ticking me off and marking my work! *Fuck you all!* If nobody can recognize what I am, fuck 'em! And Yoko too, fuckin' hell!

YOKO: That's why it's an amazing thing, after somebody who's done something like the Beatles, you'd think that he's sort of satisfied, but actually . . .

JOHN: The Beatles was nothing, it was like . . .

YOKO: . . . the Beatles situation was cutting him down into a smaller size than what he is.

JOHN: And I learned *lots* from Paul and George in many ways. But they learned a *damn sight* lot from me! They learned a *fuckin'* lot from me! And it's like George Martin or anything, just come back in twenty years' time and see what we're doing and see who's doing what. And don't mark my papers like I'm top of the maths class or did I come number one in English language, because I never did. But just assess me on what I *am* and what comes out of my mouth and what my work is, don't mark me in classrooms! It's like I've just left school again! I just *graduated* from the school of showbiz or whatever it was called.

Who do you think is good today?

[sigh]

In any art.

You see, the unfortunate thing about egomaniacs is they don't take much attention of other people's work. I only assess people on whether they're a danger to my work or not. Yoko is as important to me as Paul and Dylan rolled into one. I don't think the poor bastard will get recognition til she's dead, and there's me and maybe I could count the people on one hand that can have any *conception* of what she is or what her mind's like or what her *work* means to this *fuckin'* idiotic fuckin' generation! She has the hope that she might be recognized, but . . . If I can't get recognized, and I'm doing it in a fuckin' clown's costume, man. I'm doing it on the streets. I admire Yoko's work.

I admire Andy Warhol. I admire Zappa a bit, but I think he's a fucking intellectual. I can't think of anybody else. I admire people from the past. I admire Fellini, a few that Yoko's into. I admire Fluxus.[96] I really think what they do is beautiful and important. [Yoko has] educated me into things that I didn't know about before, just because of the scene I was in. So I'm getting to know some other *great* work that's been going on in the past and now. There's all sorts going

[96] A New York-based group of artists founded by George Macuinas.

on. But I still *love* Little Richard! And I *love* Jerry Lee Lewis! They're like primitive painters.

Chuck Berry is one of the all-time great poets, a rock poet you could call him. He was well advanced of his time lyric-wise. We all owe a lot to him, including Dylan. I've loved everything he's done, ever. He was in a different class from the other performers, he was in the tradition of the great blues artists but he really wrote his own stuff—I know Richard did, but Berry *really* wrote stuff, just the lyrics were fantastic, even though we didn't know what he was saying half the time.

YOKO: I'm really getting into it.

JOHN: We're both showing each other's experience to each other. And it's like you say when you play Yoko's music or something, I had the same thing. I had to open up to hear it. I had to get out of the concept of what I wanted to hear—to allow abstract art or music in. She had to do the same for rock & roll; it was an intellectual exercise because we're all *boxed in!* We're all in little boxes. And somebody has to come in and go—[*makes sound*] rip your fuckin' head open for you to allow something else in! A drug will do it, acid will box your head open and you think, "Fuckin' hell!" Some artists can do it, but they usually have to be dead two hundred years to do it. All I ever learned in art school was about fuckin' Van Gogh and stuff! They didn't teach me anything about anybody that was alive *now!* They never taught me about Marcel Duchamp, which I *despise* them for, and Yoko has taught me about Duchamp and what he did, which is just out of this—fantastic! He got a fuckin' bike wheel and said, "This is art, you cunts!" He wasn't Dali. Dali's alright, but he's like *Mick*.

YOKO: Well, see, you heard about Dali in school.

JOHN: No, but if you put the thing back into that age, Dali is like Mick and Duchamp is like me or you.

YOKO: Mick, yes, yes, yes, yes.

JOHN: And I love Dali, but fuckin' Duchamp was spot on!

Why Warhol?

Because—because—because—

YOKO: He's creating the same impact.

JOHN: He just . . .

He's a great original.

He's great.

YOKO: Um, great. He's an original.

JOHN: He's an original great. He's in so much *pain*, but he's got his fame, and he's got his own cinema and all that. I don't dig all that junkie fag scene and all that that he lives in. I don't know whether he lives like that or what. I dig Heinz Soup Can.[97] That was *something*! That wasn't just a pop art or some stupid ass like Peter Max and all that psychedelic *shit!*

YOKO: No, it's not that . . .

JOHN: Warhol's one of the *greats!* He said it, nobody else said it, *Heinz Soup!* He said that to us, and I thank him for it.

Fellini.

Oh, Fellini's more like Dali, I suppose . . .

YOKO: Dali, yeah.

JOHN: I mean Fellini's just great.

YOKO: We just saw that great . . .

JOHN: A great meal, to go and see Fellini's [movies]. A great meal of senses.

---

[97] Lennon is referring to Warhol's Campbell's soup can paintings.

YOKO: We like *Citizen Kane*, don't we [*laugh*]?

JOHN: And *Citizen Kane*. That's something else too. Poor old Orson [Welles], though, he was troubled. He goes on [the] Dick Cavett [Show] and he's sort of [*sadly*], "Please love me, I'm a big fat man now and I've eaten all this food and I did do well when I was younger and I can act, I can direct and you're all very kind to me but at the moment I don't do anything."

Do you see a time when you'll retire?

No, I *couldn't*, you know.

YOKO: He'll probably work until eighty or until he dies.

JOHN: Well, I don't know. I can't foresee it. Because even when you're a cripple, you carry on painting. I would paint if I couldn't move. It doesn't matter, you see. When I was saying about what Yoko did with "Greenfield Morning" and took half an inch of rubbishy tape that none of us knew what we were doing at the time, it was just a bum tape, when I saw her create something, with something we would normally throw away. With the other stuff we did, we were all good in the backing and everything went according to plan, it was a good session, but with "Greenfield Morning" and "Paper Shoes" there was nothing there for her to work with.[98] She just took nothing—the way Spector did— that's the way the genius shows through any media. You give Yoko or Spector a piece of tape, two inches of tape, they can create a symphony out of it. You don't have to be trained in rock & roll, the same as I didn't

---

98 "Greenfield Morning" and "Paper Shoes" were tracks on 1970's *Yoko Ono & Plastic Ono Band*.

have to be trained to sing. I can sing. Singing is singing til people enjoy what you sing, and not being able to hold notes or anything like that. And I don't have to do; I don't have to do it in rock & roll. If I'm an old man, I can—we'll make wallpaper together.

YOKO: [laugh]

What is holding back people understanding Yoko?

Well, she was doing alright before she met *Elvis*. When I was telling you that Howard Smith announced he was going to play her music and all these idiots rang up and said, "Don't dare play it, she split the Beatles."[99] She didn't split the Beatles. And even if she did, so what's that got to do with their fuckin' record? But she's a woman and she's Japanese, there's racial prejudice against her and there's female prejudice against her. It's as simple as that. People come up and shake my hand, they don't . . . I say, "This is my wife!"

Well, that's why they don't like Yoko.

Her work is far out. Has anybody understood Warhol really or understood his [films]—[whistle] that "building," you know, "24 hours of sleep" and that—Yoko's *Bottoms* thing is as important.[100] *Bottoms* film is as important as *Sgt. Pepper*. The real hip people, they know about it. A person in Paris knows about her, a person in Moscow knows about her, a person in fuckin' China knows about her. But in general she can't be accepted, because she's so far out, man, it's hard to take! Her pain is such that she expresses herself in a way that *hurts* you! That you cannot take it! That's why they couldn't take Van Gogh and all that shit, it's too *real*! It *hurts*! That's why they *kill* you!

---

[99] Smith was one of New York's hipper radio DJs of the time.

[100] Yoko's "Film No. 4 (Bottoms)," which she made in 1966.

What accounts for your great popularity?

Because I fuckin' did it in—I copped out in that Beatle thing. I was like an artist that went off and—like—you never heard of Dylan Thomas and all them that's never fuckin' wrote, they just went off drinkin' and Brendan Behan and all them died of drink. Everybody who's done anything is like that. I just found meself in a *party!* I was an *emperor*, and I had *millions* of chicks, drugs, drink, fuckin' *power!* And everybody sayin' how *great* I was. How could I get out of there, just— [*humming*] it was just like being in a *fucking coach!* I couldn't get *out*, I couldn't create either! I created a little, it came out, but I was in the *party*, man! You don't get out of a thing like that! it was *fantastic!* I came out of the sticks. I didn't hear about anything though—Van Gogh was the most far out thing I'd ever heard of. And even *London* was something we used to *dream* of, and London's nothing! And Paris and all this, it was all that. I came out the fucking *sticks* to take over the *fucking world*, it seemed like to me! I was *enjoying* it, and I was in it and I was *trapped* in it too. I couldn't do anything about it. I was just going along for the ride, I was *hooked. Hooked*, just like on junk.

What do you think of America?

I love it, you know, and I hate it [*laugh*].

YOKO: It's a very lovely thing, isn't it?

JOHN: America is where it's at. You know, I should have been born in New York, man, I should have been born in the Village! That's where I belong! Why wasn't I born there! Like Paris was in the eighteenth century or whatever it was, London I don't think has ever been it. It might have been it literary-wise when Wilde and Shaw and all them were there. New York was *it!* I regret *profoundly* not being *American* and not being born in Greenwich Village. That's where I should have been. But it never works that way. Everybody heads towards the center, that's why I'm here now. I'm here just to breathe it. It might be dying, or there might be a lot of dirt in the air, but this is where it's happening. And you go to Europe to rest, like in the country. But it's so overpowering, America, for me, and I'm such a fuckin' cripple that I can't take much of it, it's too much for me.

YOKO: He's very New York.

JOHN: I'm too *frightened* of it. It's so much and people are so *aggressive.* I can't take all that, you know? I need to go *home*, I need to look at the grass. I'm always writing about English garden and that lot. I need that, the trees and the grass. [*To Yoko*] Don't I?

YOKO: Yes, yes. Definitely.

JOHN: Yeah, I need to go into the country. Because I can't stand too much . . .

What is Liverpool like?

Liverpool was just where I was brought up. [It's] like anywhere . . . I love the *concept* of it, but I don't live there.

What did being from Liverpool have to do with your art?

Because it was a port, that means it was *less* hick than somewhere in the midlands, like the Midwest or whatever you call it. We were a port, the second biggest port in England. Also between Manchester and Liverpool, the North was where all the money was made in the 1800s whenever it was, that was where all the brass and the heavy people were. And that's where the despised people were. We were the ones that were looked *down* upon by the southerners as *animals*. Like the South, you, all you Easterners think that people are *pigs* down South here and the people in New York think West Coast's hick and all that. So we were hicksville, and also we were all—great amount of Irish descent and blacks and Chinamen, all sorts there—it's like San Francisco. Why do you think Haight-Ashbury and all that happened there and didn't happen in L.A.? It happened in San Francisco. That's where people are going. L.A. you pass through and get a hamburger. Liverpool was like that, but there was nothing big, it wasn't American, it was going poor. It was a very poor city and tough. But people had a sense of humor because they're in so much pain. So they're always cracking jokes, they're very witty. And it's an Irish place. It's where the Irish came when they ran out of potatoes. And it's where black people were left or worked as slaves or whatever and the trader communities. It's cosmopolitan, and it's where the sailors would come home with the blues records from America on the ships! And the biggest country & western following in England [is] in Liverpool, probably besides London— *always* besides London, because there's more of it there. I remember the first guitar I ever saw was a guy in a cowboy suit in a province of Liverpool with the stars and the cowboy hat. And a big dobro. They're real cowboys there, they take it seriously. There've been cowboys long before there was rock & roll. There's folk clubs and all that was going on there. So there's all that kind of environment.

Right after 'Sgt. Pepper,' George came to San Francisco.

George went over, in the end. I was all for going there and living on the Haight. In my head I thought, "Well, hell, acid's it and this is the answer, I'll go there." I was going to go there. But I'm too nervous to do anything actually. I thought, "Haight, I'll go there now and we'll live like that, and I'll make music and all that." But of course it didn't come true. But it happened in San Francisco, it *happened* alright, didn't it? It goes down in history. I *love* it, it's like while Shaw was in England and they all went to Paris and there's all that, and New York, San Francisco and London. Even London we created something there, with Mick and us and all of them. We didn't know what we were doing, but we were all talking and blabbing over coffee like they must have done in Paris talking about painting. We—[Eric] Burdon and Brian Jones would be up night and day talking about music and playing records and blabbing and arguing and getting drunk. It's beautiful history. It happened in all these different places. I just *missed* New York. In New York, they have their own *cool* clique. She [Yoko] came out of that. This is the first time I'm really seeing [New York], you see, cause I was always too nervous or I was a famous Beatle. Dylan showed it to me once on a sort of guided tour around the Village with him, but I never got any feel of it. I just knew *Dylan* was New York, and I always sort of wished I'd been there for the experience that Bob got, from living around it.

What's the nature of your relationship with Dylan?

Well, it's sort of acquaintance, because we're so nervous. Whenever we used to meet, it was always under the most nerve-wracking circumstances. I know I was always uptight and I know Bobby was. People like [journalist] Al Aronowitz would try and bring us together. And we were together and we'd spend some time, but I'd always be too paranoid or I'd be aggressive or something and vice versa. We didn't really speak, but we spent a lot of time together, and he came to me house, which was Kenwood, can you imagine it? And I didn't know where to put him in this sort of bourgeois home life I was living, I didn't know what to do and things like that. It was all strange. I used to go to his hotel rather. And I loved him, because he wrote some beautiful stuff. I used to love his so-called protest things. But I like the sound of him. I didn't have to listen to his words. He used to come with his acetate and say, [imitates Dylan] "Listen to this, John." And "Did you hear the words?" And I said, "That doesn't matter, just the sound is what counts. The overall thing." You didn't have to hear what Bob Dylan's saying, you just have to hear the way he says it, like medium is the message, all—whatever mix of—but Dylan was like that. But I had quite a good . . .

YOKO: But you respect him a lot.

JOHN: . . . I respected him, I respect him a lot. I know Paul didn't. I think Paul was jealous. Paul didn't like any other artist. But that's valid. Paul didn't get hyped by me. I had too many father figures.

YOKO: And you like words . . .

JOHN: I like words too, so I liked a lot of the stuff he did. I like words.

Do you see him as the great artist?

No, I see him as another poet, or as competition. You just read my books, which are written before I'd heard of Dylan or read Dylan or even heard of anybody, it's the *same*. I didn't come after Elvis and Dylan, I've been around always. But if I see or meet a great artist, I love 'em. I just love 'em, I go fanatical about them for a short period, and then I get over it. And if they wear green socks, I'm liable to wear green socks for a period, too.

When was the last time you saw Bob?

He came to our house with George when I'd written "Cold Turkey" and we were . . .

YOKO: And his wife.

JOHN: . . . and his wife—I was just trying again to put him on piano for "Cold Turkey" to make a rough take, but his wife was pregnant or something and they left. But he's calmed down a lot now than what he was. I just remember we were both in shades and both on fucking junk. And all these freaks around us, and Ginsberg and all those people. I was nervous as shit.

Where did this happen?

In London when he came.

You were in that movie with him.[101]

Oh yeah, I've never seen it. I'm in it. Frightened as hell.

I haven't seen it but somebody told me about it.

I'd love to see it. I have to see it. I must ask to see it.

YOKO: How could we see it? Could you arrange it?

Sure.

YOKO: Oh great!

JOHN: I never did see it. I was so frightened, you know. I was always so paranoid that Bob said, "I want you to be in this film." He just wanted me to be in the film. I thought, "Why? What? He's going to put me down!" I went all through this terrible thing. So in the film, I'm just blabbing off [and], I'm commenting all the time, like you do when you're very high and stoned. Yeah. What did he say?

I don't remember the exact thing, but you come off really nervous.

Yeah. So . . .

YOKO: I'd like to see it.

JOHN: . . . I'd been up all night.

You were trying to trade humor?

Yeah. That's it. We were being smart alecks. Oh, it's terrible. But it was *his* scene. That was the problem for me. It was *his* movie and I was

---

[101] D.A. Pennebaker's *Eat the Document*, filmed in 1966.

on his territory. That's why I was so nervous. I was on *his* session.

YOKO: Tomorrow night?

JOHN: No, Yoko, we've got—you're going to see the Toronto rock film tomorrow, you're going to make a film tomorrow and you're going to do an interview tomorrow, and you probably lined up Howard Smith for tomorrow by the sound of what you were saying on the bloody phone. [*Points to Yoko*] This is the woman who drove me mad.

YOKO: [*laugh*]

JOHN: [*laugh*] No. Yeah. Okay? So try and cool it. We'll see it some other day. But if you can just tell us how to get in touch with it, that would be interesting.

It's Pennebaker.

Oh yeah. Oh, I see, okay, well we'll probably see him tomorrow. I don't know how we're going to see it *and* make a movie. I mean it's such a full day.

YOKO: We better get going.

JOHN: Well, we better go and copy this tape, anyway cause I want it all for the archives.

[*on the phone a week or so later*]

You're going back to London. What's a rough picture of your immediate future, say, the next three months?

I'd like to just vanish a bit. It wore me out, New York. I love it. I'm just sort of fascinated by it, like a fucking monster. Doing the films was a nice way of meeting a lot of people. I think we've both said and done enough for a few months, especially with this article. I'd like to get out of the way and wait til they all . . .

Do you have a rough picture of the next few years?

Oh no, I couldn't think of the next few years; it's abysmal thinking of how many years there are to go, millions of them. I just play it by the week. I don't think much ahead of a week.

I have no more to ask.

Well, fancy that.

Do you have anything to add?

No, I can't think of anything positive and heartwarming to win your readers over.

Do you have a picture of "When I'm 64"?

No, no. I hope we're a nice old couple living off the coast of Ireland or something like that, looking at our scrapbook of madness.

3764578 hill